Tightrope Walk:
Identity, Survival and the
Corporate World in African American Literature

Tightrope Walk

*Identity, Survival and
the Corporate World in
African American Literature*

James Robert Saunders

McFarland & Company, Inc., Publishers
Jefferson, North Carolina, and London

British Library Cataloguing-in-Publication data are available

Library of Congress Cataloguing-in-Publication Data

Saunders, James Robert, 1953–
    Tightrope walk : identity, survival and the corporate world
in African American literature / James Robert Saunders.
        p.   cm.
    Includes bibliographical references and index.
    ISBN 0-7864-0358-6 (library binding : 55# alkaline paper) ∞
    1. American literature — Afro-American authors — History and
criticism.   2. American literature — 20th century — History and
criticism.   3. Identity (Psychology) in literature.   4. Group
identity in literature.   5. Afro-Americans in literature.   6. Race
relations in literature.   7. Corporations in literature.   8. Afro-
Americans — Employment.   9. Survival in literature.   I. Title.
PS153.N5S28   1997
810.9'896073 — dc21   96-47867
                                                                CIP

Manufactured in the United States of America

*McFarland & Company, Inc., Publishers
Box 611, Jefferson, North Carolina 28640*

For

Renae and Mudda,
rocks in a sea of trouble,

Monica,
who is fast becoming a boulder,

and the aunts —
*Beatrice, Dulcenia, Evelyn, Irene,
Lillian* and *Sadie,*
pillars of strength who
influenced me while I traveled along my way

Table of Contents

Acknowledgments

I am deeply indebted to Joanne L. Hartough's Interlibrary Loans Department at the Carlson Library on the University of Toledo's Bancroft Campus. Also, the Reference and Circulation Departments at that library consistently rendered me valuable advice in my search for various materials.

As I was in the final stages of preparing this manuscript, it just so happens that I was involved in circumstances strangely reminiscent of those endured by the fictional character Benjamin "Chappie" Puttbutt who I analyze in the book's fourth chapter. I am grateful to all who supported me, but most especially Christine Child, Mildred A. Tipton, Thomas R. Lopez, and Matthew H. Wikander.

Thanks also to William A. Elwood and William M. Harris, at the University of Virginia, and Richard W. Bailey and Joseph L. Blotner, at the University of Michigan, for crucial advice in the early years.

Preface

At a recent dinner honoring Henry Louis Gates, the topic of law schools came up whereupon he and I discovered that we had much more in common than just our interest in literary criticism. He had attended Yale Law School for about a month in the early 1970s before dropping out. I, a few years later, had graduated from Harvard Law School but had found the experience to be utterly depressing. I expressed my admiration for the courage he displayed in leaving as soon as he discovered that a legal career was not what he wanted. He in return conveyed admiration for me that I had stayed and finished out the program even after learning that law was not what I wanted either.

"Why did you stay?" he asked me, to which I responded, "A person doesn't come out of my circumstances, go off to a place like the Harvard Law School, and then show up a week later on his Ma's back porch, tail between his legs, talking about how he couldn't cut the mustard." I went on to tell him about my fatherless childhood, hardworking mother, and an assortment of other details that comprise the nuts and bolts of my youth. With typical perceptiveness, Gates answered me back with a simple, "I bet there's more to it than that." We must have both felt the intensity of the subsequent silence and nothing more was said on the subject. But he had been absolutely right. There was so much more involved with my decision to stay than merely not wanting to embarrass my mother, however proud she had been at my having been accepted at the distinguished Cambridge institution.

The real reason I stayed had to do with the waging of a battle that I had undertaken on my very first day of law school classes when I encountered my own Professor Kingsfield (the crusty old professor in John Jay Osborn's novel *The Paper Chase*) who could make students cringe with his simple request that they state the facts of a legal case. The first time I was called on to state the case in Philip Areeda's "Contracts" class, I was stunned in exactly the same way that Hart was in Osborn's now classic tale of law school misadventure.

1

When Hart, seat 259, heard his name, he froze. Caught unprepared, he simply stopped functioning. Then he felt his heart beat faster than he could ever remember its beating and his palms [broke] out in a sweat.[1]

As in Hart's situation, I discovered too late that the assignment we were expected to have completed by the first day of class had been posted on an obscure bulletin board a few days before class had begun. No introduction of students. No easing into the material. Just a headlong plunge into the Socratic method, that process of teaching whereby the instructor posits hypothetical situations for students, called on at random, to decipher.

Not all of my classes were conducted in this manner. But I came to regard my "Contracts" class as the real test of my abilities as a potential lawyer. A rather famous classmate of mine Scott Turow, in his memoir *One L* (the nickname for first-year law school students), expressed his own reservations about the law school educational process and explained what I have only now come to comprehend as a prevailing sense of student insecurity. Turow wrote:

Harvard Law School was a place where only merit, only raw intelligence and perseverance ... were the sole means of success. Increasingly, I'd become certain that I was short on both counts.... I had nothing worth saying in class. I made *mistakes*—in fact, silly blunders. If lucky, I was mediocre.[2]

Quite the contrary, of course, Turow is brilliant as his novels and legal career readily attest. So what is it about law school that makes the majority of its students so doubtful? At Harvard, about 550 students make up each year's entering class. The 550 are divided into four sections composed of about 138 students each. Each section of students attends the same classes together in what Turow accurately refers to as a "tiny universe ... a dense and hectic orbit" within which practically all of your relationships have been predetermined.

It is this factor that gives the law school its factory-like aura, with we the students being processed like so many widgets to be received in the end by a corporate world. Fancying myself as something of a unique personality, I resisted the process, at least as it was administered by Areeda. After my first day of being unprepared, students began stopping me in the hallways and calling me on the phone with suggestions on how to get into the classroom intellectual fray. "Raise your hand as soon as possible. Volunteer!" was their common plea. And the thought occurred to me to do just that: prepare as thoroughly as I could and then volunteer to answer questions. But something possessed me instead to go in the opposite direction, "passing" (that is, refusing to answer questions in class) until Areeda no longer called on me for anything. And when concerned classmates questioned me with regard to what I was doing, I merely responded, "I don't believe the Socratic method is the best way for me to learn the law."

In further explanation, I could have told them that my interests would have been better served in a small classroom setting or in independent study courses where I could chart my own direction while I mastered the relevant legal material. But even more importantly, I was tired. Born in the segregated South, I could never shake the sense of being a cog in the machinery of some onerously noble experiment. Stepping out of the shadows of a nurturing black elementary school, I had been thrust into the midst of a white junior high school, and then on to a white high school. When it came time for me to select a college, I was so used to integrating one thing or another that I volunteered to go to the University of Virginia and survived there mainly because of the independent studies, the self-devised programs, a few professors who understood me, and the knowledge I had that at any given moment I could retreat into a self-discovering seclusion and pop out only when I wanted to do so, establishing associations with whomever I wished as I went about the process of trying to create my identity.

When I applied to law school in the fall of 1974, I was totally unaware that there were altogether only three black lawyers who had reached the rank of partner in the major law firms in New York City. Actually I had no idea what a law firm was or that New York, and Wall Street in particular, was the entrepreneurial center of the United States. William Elwood, my English professor and undergraduate mentor, did everything he could to guide me in the direction of certain realities. "Have you gone to see *The Paper Chase*?" he asked on one occasion. "Can you come to my house tomorrow evening?" he asked me on another. In that latter instance, he introduced me to a former Charlottesville mayor's son who was a lawyer and who, as it turns out, did not make a strong impression in terms of recommending the legal field. That should have told me something right there. But by then I was already determined to go to law school, basing my intentions on some Perry Mason-like ideal that I concluded was what lawyering was all about.

Upon graduating from Harvard, I decided to return to my birthplace — Richmond, Virginia — where I thought I might get reacquainted with myself. Now I was totally disenchanted with law and I applied instead for trust management positions at the local banks, and was told in more than one interview that I would be "president of the bank one day." As a 25-year-old black man, I did not fully comprehend the nature of my own discomfort as I listened to that prediction from my interviewers. But 17 years later, I would experience the same stinging discomfort as I read Bebe Moore Campbell's *Brothers and Sisters* and listened while Humphrey Boone's interviewer declared, "I am in a position to make a promise: If you accept my offer and if you do the job that I believe you're capable of, I'll groom you for the presidency."[3] A generous offer indeed until one realizes that for a black man, the "capability" to which the interviewer refers will have more to do with certain ancillary factors than with the quality of Boone's job performance. He will have to adhere strictly to the corporate dress code; he must be self-effacing at opportune moments; he must talk using "clipped enunciation and perfect diction"; and above all else, if he is attracted to a white woman, he must learn to stifle those feelings. It is Boone's "failure" in this latter requirement that ultimately results in his undoing, for as discreet as he had intended to be, his interest in white coworker Mallory Post comes to the attention of those who seek desperately to undermine him. His mask, the quintessential metaphor for deceptiveness on the part of African Americans, had not been held firmly enough in place.

William Covington, in Brent Wade's *Company Man*, experiences virtually the same dilemma. Once an obscure speechwriter for Varitech Industries, Inc., he is put on the corporate fast track and soon becomes Director of Marketing Communications. It seems like quite an accomplishment until we learn that marketing communications is a "not entirely necessary part of the business." He is expendable depending on how well he does or does not perform certain tasks that have nothing to do with marketing and everything to do with presenting the image, however false, that blacks can rise to the highest levels of management at Varitech.

He is exactly like Naylor's "second in command" (*Bailey's Cafe*) at Waco Glass and Tile. The title "second in command" sounds even more prestigious than Director of Marketing Communications, that is until we learn that the second in command presides over a rather ambiguous department, "layout and design," within which he is the only employee. Rather than the head of a legitimate department, the second in command's real function is similar to the window-dressing capacity which Covington serves. While interviewing for a position with Waco Glass and Tile, Stanley Maple is urged by the white interviewer "to have lunch with him and another good man working in the company."[4] The good man is of course the so-called second in command who must always be available for this sort of company duty. He has no say-so in the matter of who will be hired, but he must nonetheless be there to applaud company efforts in spite of its poor record in terms of minority hiring.

Naylor, in her earlier novel *Linden Hills*, had given us another version of the second in command. Dartmouth alumnus Maxwell Smyth is the assistant to the executive director of General Motors, the assistant who "spent every waking moment trying to be no color at all."[5] Racially colorblind might be another way of characterizing that to which Smyth aspires. It may also be the politically correct stance to take in a corporate setting where ability to fit in is a crucial factor when it comes to receiving raises and promotions. Indeed, Smyth may not so much want to be colorless exactly as he just wants to do whatever is required to advance. As the critic Margaret Homans explains, "In the world of corporate America, the absence of color *is* whiteness, because neutrality is impossible where hierarchical thinking prevails."[6] Regardless of what he says, Smyth must be cognizant of the fact that for a black man to be "no color at all" is tantamount to a rejection of blackness and an acceptance of both whiteness and the prevailing social order. But that is the price he is willing to pay, selling his soul for a place in a system that nevertheless subjugates the masses of African Americans.

In her autobiography *Volunteer Slavery*, Jill Nelson recounts her experiences as a writer for *The Washington Post* where she refused to play the role of lackey doing the bidding for a racially insensitive master. In 1986, the *Post* inaugurated a magazine section for its Sunday edition and hired Nelson as the first African American on that magazine's staff. Having previously been a freelance writer for periodicals such as *Essence* and *The Village Voice*, she nevertheless ventured from New York City to Washington, D.C. with all the optimism of someone embarking on an exciting new career opportunity.

What she learns upon her arrival, however, is that it is not so much important to her supervisors that she produce articles for the magazine as it is important for her to support the views of those writers whose work does find its way into the magazine's pages. She is expected to perform exactly like Naylor's second in command and Wade's Bill Covington, those other black employees who were hired neither to provide true diversity nor to be independent thinkers. Rather, by hiring African Americans, those companies merely hope to obtain the type of minority who will blindly support current policy.

As it turns out, the world of academia is not all that different from how many corporations conduct their affairs. One college professor, Jay Parini, has even gone so far as to put into print, in *The Chronicle of Higher Education*, what those of us in higher education always knew to be the truth. Fearful of the inherent dangers, Parini urges untenured faculty to "keep their mouths shut" until however long it takes them to get tenured. Tenure can be denied, though it is never stated this way, simply because a person is perceived as not fitting in, not a part of the "good old boy" network.

In his novel *Japanese by Spring*, Ishmael Reed examines just such a situation as he shows the African American Professor Benjamin Puttbutt opposing such policies as affirmative action and divestment from South Africa. Puttbutt expects that his reward will be tenure. By the end of *Company Man*, Wade's Covington has actually been split into separate schizophrenic personalities as a consequence of trying to meet the demands of his employment. Puttbutt however goes one step further, at one point even eliminating his African American consciousness totally, putting his

> black days ... behind him. He no longer suffered from the double consciousness that Du Bois spoke of. The black part of him had been completely annihilated. His photo could appear on a box of Wheaties and nobody would know the difference.[7]

Not that Puttbutt is light-skinned enough to "pass" for white; but he has denied his blackness in the psychological sense. And as his photograph can now appear on a Wheaties box without it ever being clear that he is black, we witness not only the eradication of a race identity but an elimination also of the very foundation upon which he might have been respected as a human being.

Which brings us to *Invisible Man*, and as Ellison states in the prologue of that novel, "The end is in the beginning and lies far ahead." So though I, in my preface, have reserved Ellison's novel as the last to be mentioned, within its pages lies the underlying, unifying theme for my book. It is thus apropos that this novel is the subject of my initial chapter. "I am," asserts Ellison's inscrutable narrator, "invisible ... simply because people refuse to see me." Others cannot see him, but neither is the narrator able to discern his own identity, so powerful are the forces that would have him remain an anonymous entity. Such is the nature of the battle that I spoke about earlier, the one that required me to stay at Harvard in spite of how much I abhorred the curriculum. Having been so obviously relegated to the status of a mere number (and then told that I should think a certain way) left me with no choice but to stay an object, for while it is one thing to remain hidden in what one presumes to be the knowledge of himself, it is quite another thing — and indeed perhaps necessary — to come out and test that identity.

If the narrator in *Invisible Man* had never gone to the college, he might never have begun the process that led him to encounters with the treacherous Bledsoe, the manipulative Brotherhood, and the brutally demanding Ras the Exhorter. If he had stayed in his hole, he might never have found his identity; he might never have had to pit his own ideals against the forces that wage a never ending battle for conformity.

In *Invisible Man* we observe a college functioning as the obedient appendage of a philanthropic corporation. In fact, the boards of trustees of most colleges and universities adhere to the corporate model. And so it should not be surprising to see institutions of higher learning becoming quasi-corporate entities where success is measured not in terms of academic freedom but instead by the power of autocratic rule. Numbers are the main priority: number of students, number of buildings, number of publications, number of dollars. And the challenge, in the midst of all that bureaucracy and blind allegiance to the norm, will be to save something of our true selves, to shed some light for a later generation who will undoubtedly find itself enmeshed in a war for its very soul.

Young Mr. Emerson's Crucial Message: "All Our Motives Are Impure"

It was during the summer of 1971 that I was first introduced to Ralph Ellison's extraordinary novel *Invisible Man*. I was about to enter my first year of college and was enrolled in a preparatory program designed for African American students who were deemed not quite up to snuff for regular admission to the prestigious University of Virginia. Houston Baker was a recently hired associate professor and he visited one of our evening sessions to talk about *Invisible Man*. But he talked very little about that novel, and what he did say focused mainly on the character, young Mr. Emerson.

The edition of the novel that we were using was 568 pages, and the section in which young Emerson appears, comprised only 13 of all those pages. Prior to Baker's presentation, I had deemed Emerson all but insignificant. I could barely recall him when that professor first mentioned his name. Then Baker asked us what our assessment was of the fact that Emerson touched the narrator on his knee. I was baffled. First of all, I did not even remember that incident. And if he did touch the narrator on his knee, so what? People touch each other inadvertently in all kinds of ways. But as Baker smiled and raised his eyebrows, there was the subtle suggestion of something else involved in Emerson's act. None of us students caught the hint at that time, and it would be a full decade later before I understood exactly where our classroom visitor was leading us.

Now, as I gloss over the 13 Emerson-related pages, I recognize the hints that Ellison himself supplied with regard to homosexuality. Seeking to identify with the narrator's plight of being African American, Emerson confides:

What I want to do is done very seldom, and, to be honest, it wouldn't
happen now if I hadn't sustained a series of impossible frustrations.
You see — well, I'm a thwarted . . . Oh, damn, there I go again,
thinking only of myself ... We're both frustrated, understand?
Both of us, and I want to help you ... but there is a tyranny
involved.[1]

Words such as "thwarted" and "frustrated" clue us in to the fact that
young Emerson is a homosexual who has not been allowed the freedom
to publicly affirm his sexual identity. When he speaks of there being a
"tyranny involved," he has specific reference to his father, the prominent businessman who in all likelihood has made silence in the matter
a condition of his son's employment. "Identity!" young Emerson
exclaims at one point, "My God! Who has any identity any more ...?"[2]
His father is a tyrant, but in a larger sense, society as a whole has stifled
the expression of this sort of sexual identity. It is society that has deemed
homosexuality deviant and exacted retribution accordingly.

Authors writing in the 1950s and earlier had to be careful about
how they presented homosexual issues. They generally were not allowed
to be explicit. We will recall how J. D. Salinger, in *The Catcher in the
Rye*, renders subtle hints about the identity of Mr. Antolini. In that
book, Antolini calls the main protagonist "handsome" and, says the
narrator, "He was sitting on the floor right next to the couch, in the dark
and all, and he was sort of petting me or patting me on the goddam
head."[3] The distinction between "petting" and "patting" is presented
for our consideration and then intentionally blurred even as we are trying to determine the significance of Antolini in terms of his relationship with Holden Caulfield.

What we do know is that the presumed homosexual in Salinger's
novel wants identification with another who, like him, is a quintessential outsider. The older man (Antolini) becomes a mentor for the
younger man (Caulfield) who had thought of education as a phony
enterprise. Antolini, on the other hand, urges his advisee to consider
how a formal education can

begin to give you an idea what size mind you have. What it'll fit
and, maybe, what it won't.... it may save you an extraordinary
amount of time trying on ideas that don't suit you.... You'll begin to
know your true measurements and dress your mind accordingly.[4]

Antolini does not attempt to dissuade Caulfield from his belief that
people and institutions are phony. He merely wants to help Caulfield

survive in the midst of the chaos and hypocrisy. The older man had already witnessed the "suicide" of another idealist, James Castle, who refused to budge from his stance against phoniness. Castle called Phil Stabile a "very conceited guy," and, as Caulfield conveys it, when Stabile and "about six" of his buddies confronted Castle, he "jumped out the window" rather than retract his accurate characterization.

It is significant that Castle dies wearing Caulfield's sweater. Salinger evidently wants us to consider Castle as Caulfield's alter ego. And then when we also consider that Castle's initials are "J. C.," we are brought to the realization that he is Christ-like in some ways. Recalling the time when Castle had asked to borrow his sweater, Caulfield notes, "I didn't even know he knew I *had* a turtleneck sweater."[5] The quiet, unassuming Castle is more perceptive than most, perhaps even to the point of having supernatural abilities. And he holds fast to truth even in the face of impending dire consequences.

Caulfield is not as much the Christ-like figure as Castle. He is supremely capable of superficiality and phoniness. He judges women based on their physical appearance, pretends to know people he has only met once, he lies about his name and on one occasion concocts a long, rambling story of praise about a classmate he actually despises. He tells Mrs. Morrow that her son is so modest that he declined the nomination for class president when what Caulfield really thinks is that her son, Ernest, is the "biggest bastard that ever went to Pencey, in the whole crummy history of the school."[6] In other words, Caulfield knows exactly what to say and do in certain of life's more complicated situations, and by the end of the novel he may even have reconciled himself with the reality of lying as essential to human existence.

As with Salinger's novel, *Invisible Man* has its end at the beginning with a narrator who recapitulates the chain of events that led him to greater self-knowledge. Though Caulfield appears to learn his life lessons quicker, the invisible man does know enough to correct himself when he lets the phrase "social equality" slip out as he is speaking before the "town's leading white citizens." Yet he does not know enough to tell a lie instead of taking Mr. Norton out to the countryside where he will encounter the incestuous Jim Trueblood. Trueblood of course is the last person in the world that the college president, Bledsoe, would want the trustee to meet, and the invisible man is left defending himself arduously, insisting, "I only stopped there after he ordered me to."[7] Bledsoe rails back at him:

> Ordered you? ... Dammit, white folks are always giving orders, it's a
> habit with them. Why didn't you make an excuse? ... Why that
> Trueblood shack? My God, boy! You're black and living in the
> South — did you forget how to lie?[8]

In Bledsoe's mind, the narrator's mistake is unforgivable. That college
president is prototypical in the sense that he knows what his predicament is, having to persuade white philanthropists that his institution
accedes to their wishes. Indeed, Bledsoe is not above singing a spiritual
or two when the occasion demands it, particularly if it means that the
institution's coffers will benefit from his presentation.

The invisible man, through his carelessness, has jeopardized the
mission of the school, and the president's punishment is swift. "I can't
possibly let this pass," Bledsoe declares. "Boy, I'm getting rid of you!"[9]
The narrator threatens back, "I'll go to Mr. Norton and tell him.... I'll
tell everybody. I'll fight you. I swear it, I'll fight!"[10] This is when Bledsoe backs down a bit and takes a different approach to dealing with his
game young charge. The president feigns humble submission, but
remains imperceptible as far as his intentions are concerned. After
advising the narrator to go to New York for the summer to "earn [his]
next year's fees," he cannily gives him seven letters of recommendation
and pretends that they will aid him in getting a job. He instructs:

> These letters will be sealed; don't open them if you want help.
> White folk are strict about such things. The letters will introduce
> you and request them to help you with a job. I'll do my best for you
> and it isn't necessary for you to open them, understand?[11]

The invisible man accepts the president's stipulation and will be shocked
once he learns that the recommendations are not at all supportive of his
efforts to get a job, but are designed instead to thwart any of his attempts
at that endeavor. Bledsoe's plot is a type of treachery for which our
naive narrator is ill-prepared. Indeed there is no telling how long he
might have continued distributing the false recommendations before
realizing what was really going on.

It is young Mr. Emerson who shares with our narrator the contents
of Bledsoe's recommendation. And thus in a novel that is full of names
that are intrinsically significant, we must consider what the name
"Emerson" means. The author (Ralph Waldo Ellison) was himself
named after Ralph Waldo Emerson, the nineteenth century poet-
philosopher particularly famous for the essay "Self-Reliance" where he

urges, "Trust thyself. Whoso would be a man must be a noncon-formist.... Nothing is at last sacred but the integrity of your own mind."[12] This is the lesson that Ellison's narrator must learn, for in a world where people's motives are at best unclear, one must develop keen instincts and then rely on those instincts for survival especially when circumstances descend to the depths of absurdity.

In his essay, "Hidden Name and Complex Fate," Ellison tells of his own boyhood and the time he found a lens that he could not figure out how to use. Later in the essay, Ellison uses that lens as a metaphor for his own rather elaborate name, confiding, "I could no more deal with my name — I shall never really master it — than I could find a creative use for my lens."[13] Ellison admitted to a certain fascination with the act of naming and the "magic involved" when one hits upon a name that has profound "suggestive powers." With a name like Ralph Waldo Elli-son, derived as it was from a great literary figure from the not-so-dis-tant past, one can imagine the challenge thus incumbent upon the later writer in the process of self-definition.

James Alan McPherson is helpful in this regard. Writing in 1970 for *The Atlantic Monthly*, he comments on how

> Ellison seems to have very limited contact with the black writers who also live there [New York]. Yet his shadow lies over all their writers' conferences, and his name is likely to be invoked, and defamed, by any number of the participants at any conference. One man has said that he would like to shoot Ellison.[14]

McPherson further describes the ambivalence of black students at col-leges such as Oberlin, Tougaloo, and Iowa State when Ellison came to speak. One went so far as to call him an "Uncle Tom." In an era where slogans such as "black power" and "black is beautiful" predominated, Ellison seems to have treaded upon an ambiguous middle ground rem-iniscent of the preacher's admonition (in *Invisible Man*'s prologue) that "black will make you ... or black will un-make you."[15] The intangible, mandated characteristic of blackness is a nevertheless vital part of the African American panorama. But Ellison goes beyond the mere con-struct of race in laying groundwork for how a search for identity might be conducted.

In his second collection of essays, *Going to the Territory*, Ellison denounces the process whereby "Americans tend to focus on the diverse parts of their culture (with which they can more easily identify) rather than on its complex and pluralistic wholeness."[16] The artist seeks the means whereby universality can be confirmed, a perspective essential to *Invisible Man* where the author concludes, "Who knows but that, on the lower frequencies, I speak for you?"[17] The profound suggestion is that he speaks for other races as well as blacks. In fact, scientists are coming more and more to accept that race is not a viable means of distinguishing human beings at all. Sharon Begley, in a *Newsweek* article, informs us that 50 per cent of physical anthropologists and 70 per cent of cultural anthropologists "reject race as a biological category."[18] Her statistics are derived from a 1989 survey conducted at Central Michigan University.

It has only been through a lengthy and generally corrupt socialization process that racial delineations have remained intact. In his essay "A Forgotten Prototype: 'The Autobiography of an Ex-Colored Man' and 'Invisible Man,'" Houston Baker points out certain similarities between Ellison's novel and James Weldon Johnson's African American classic, published 40 years earlier.[19] In *Ex-Coloured Man*, we find the nameless narrator lamenting because he is "forced to take his outlook on all things, not from the view-point of a citizen, or a man, or even a human being, but from the view-point of a *coloured* man."[20] It might be argued that nothing is wrong with the narrower view, for if one cannot appreciate his own uniquely African American perspective, is not that the equivalent of racial self-hatred?

It is worthwhile to contemplate, once again, Ellison's name — Ralph Waldo — and ponder the extent to which he may actually have been forced, by the "suggestive power" of that name to render his analysis of the African American experience in broader terms than what was typical of the times. He must have been familiar with the essay "Experience" where his 19th century namesake argued that

> life is a series of surprises, and would not be worth taking or keeping, if it were not. All good conversation, manners, and action, come from a spontaneity which forgets usages, and makes the moment great. Nature hates calculators; her methods are saltatory and impulsive. Man lives by pulses; our organic movements are such; and the chemical and ethereal agents are undulatory and alternate; and the mind goes antagonizing on, and never prospers but by fits.[21]

Earlier in the essay Emerson characterizes the masses as being like millers at the lower level of a stream. Only, there is no more water because the "upper people must have raised their dams."[22] Of course the "upper people," as Emerson uses the term, has reference to those who would deign consider it appropriate to dictate the thinking of other human beings. Meanwhile, Emerson hailed the genius in all of us and thought it more appropriate for people to think for themselves, fathom their own world views based on their own life experiences. These experiences need not be homogeneous or even decipherable in terms of their ultimate significance. But uncertainty adds to excitement, and even this presumed difficulty should not be underestimated in the process of applying individualistic meaning.

What exactly should we make of young Mr. Emerson who entreats the narrator, "We're both frustrated, understand? Both of us, and I want to help you." Later in that same exchange, he asks, "Will you trust me?" And yet again he will seek to gain the invisible man's confidence, declaring, "You mustn't believe that I'm against you … or your race. I'm your friend."[23] The invisible man is understandably skeptical of these urgings from a white stranger in pursuit of a personal relationship. And we as readers are skeptical not just of Emerson but also of Ellison's suggestion that the injustices suffered by homosexuals are similar to those suffered by African Americans.

Young Emerson invites the narrator to join him and some friends for a party at Club Calamus, a phenomenal invitation for the 1930s. Emerson asserts, "It might help you." Nevertheless, the narrator quickly declines, wanting instead to keep their relationship one that is strictly business.

Emerson has touched the narrator on his knee, invited him to a party, and inquired as to whether or not he was an athlete in college. When our narrator answers that last query with an abrupt "No sir," Emerson first examines him "up and down" and then remarks, "You have the build.... You'd probably make an excellent runner, a sprinter."[24] The dialogue is reminiscent of Walt Whitman's provocative poem "Earth, My Likeness":

Earth, my likeness,
Though you look so impassive, ample and spheric there,
I now suspect that is not all;
I now suspect there is something fierce in you eligible to burst
    forth,
For an athlete is enamour'd of me, and I of him,
But toward him there is something fierce and terrible in me
    eligible to burst forth,
I dare not tell it in words, not even in these songs.[25]

One might be tempted to argue that this is a poem merely about nature or about male comradeship in general. But it is more specifically a poem about male homosexual love. Other Whitman poems such as "To a Western Boy" and "City of Orgies" attest to this basic theme. Upon examining the last lines of "What Think You I Take My Pen in Hand?" the message becomes even clearer as Whitman acknowledges that his concern is not for cities or battleships or "splendors of the past day," but instead he is concerned about "two simple men/The one to remain hung on the other's neck and passionately kiss'd him/While the one to depart tightly prest the one to remain in his arms."[26] What we have here, and in all of the aforementioned Whitman poems, is perhaps the most daring exploration of homosexuality that could have been rendered publicly in mid-nineteenth century America. It should not be lost on us either that those poems, and others quite similar in content, comprise the "Calamus" section of *Leaves of Grass*. Recall that "Calamus" is the name of the club where young Emerson wishes the narrator to join him.

Writing in 1993, psychologist Jo Ann Lee comments on disadvantages suffered by homosexual men in the work place:

> Networking and social contacts are often instrumental to a person's climb up the ladder of success in the world of work. This avenue may be blocked or closed to the gay man.... Rapport with coworkers and superiors is often built on social commonalities such as sports or vacations. Such rapport often leads to business contacts and access to important information related to the job. Gay men have two alternatives ... create a fictional heterosexual life or abstain from social events with coworkers and superiors.[27]

If, generally speaking, this is what the situation is for homosexuals in the contemporary American business culture, then one can imagine how difficult it was for homosexuals in the work place decades ago. Coming out of the closet was not an option; the pretense of heterosexuality was the more viable choice. But what were the psychological consequences? If homosexuality was (and still is, to a large extent) regarded as a sin, what possibilities existed for homosexuals to be reconciled with their true identities? This is the state of affairs that presages young Emerson's anguish, causing him to conclude bitterly, "Who has any identity any more anyway?"

In a sense, young Emerson is more fortunate than other homosexuals, most of whom do not have a wealthy father who can provide them with an adequate job. On the other hand, Emerson might have it harder since the tyrant father is ever present, making it so that the son must venture out beyond family and job, in search of emotional support. This is why the Club Calamus is so important. It is a substitute for the social outlet that he, but for his homosexuality, would have had access to with company coworkers. In suggesting that our narrator visit the club, he offers the prospect that blackness can be equated with homosexuality in terms of what might be an alternative social outlet for both of the marginalized groups.

Putting aside, for the moment, that Emerson's offer might be a sexual advance, let us consider why else our narrator sees fit to decline the invitation. It will be useful for this purpose to look at the real-life *Clarence B. Cain v. Joel Hyatt* legal case, heard in the eastern district of Pennsylvania in 1990. The case concerned a Philadelphia-based law firm employee who was in essence fired because he had AIDS. In deciding for Cain, the court ruled that he was handicapped and should not have been fired since the handicap was not job-related. The entire time that I attended college at the University of Virginia with Clarence, I never knew he was gay. We socialized together, took classes together, and when it came time for me to choose a law school to attend, he gave me crucial advice. That he was able to hide himself so well in "the closet" for so many years is a statement in itself about the ostracism that must be endured by those who openly acknowledge their homosexual orientation.

As disturbed as I was about how Clarence died in abject poverty, having poured all his resources into the fight against Hyatt, I was even more bothered by the subsequent movie *Philadelphia*. As brilliant as Tom Hanks was, I found myself wondering why the black actor Denzel Washington had not been given the role of the AIDS-stricken lawyer. He could have delivered a performance just as good as Hanks'. And then one day in early 1994, as I was reading *The Washington Post*, I got an answer to my question. There in the "Style" section of the newspaper, the film's director Jonathan Demme issued the assurance, "We bent over backwards *not* to make it like the Cain case. To copy an existing situation — you could be subject to a lawsuit."[28] While that may sound like a good explanation, there was perhaps something else behind the decision to make the Cain-type character white. If that AIDS-stricken lawyer in the movie had been African American, the issue of homosexuality and indeed the issue of AIDS itself would have, of necessity, been pushed into the background as the predominant issue shifted to the matter of race.

And thus it is as young Emerson attempts to draw parallels between his own life and that of our narrator. Walt Whitman, in his poem "To a Stranger," has two men meet by chance, vow their love for one another, and then mold a mutual identification.[29] In Ellison's novel, young Emerson contemplates a similar process as he asks the narrator, "Do you believe that two people, two strangers who have never seen one another before can speak with utter frankness and sincerity?"[30] Whitman's two strangers were white. In *Invisible Man*, one is black, the other is white, and that makes all the difference.

Instead of someone with whom the narrator can identify, it is more appropriate to think of young Emerson as a facilitator of racial oppression. In his essay "The American Scholar," Ralph Waldo Emerson warned that "young men of the fairest promise ... are hindered from action by the disgust which the principles on which business is managed inspire."[31] If, as that philosopher believed, people can be characterized as embroiled in a conflict between idealistic and materialistic values, then we must acknowledge just how far short the novel's young Emerson falls in terms of offering us resolution. His father does not even bother to come out and meet the narrator. That northern philanthropist epitomizes self-reliance, but it is a self-reliance for which the philosopher Emerson would have had utter disdain. The father perceives self-reliance only in terms of economic gain, and the son is helpless against the inherently racist capitalistic tide.

It might be argued that the older Emerson is not primarily to blame, that in ignoring the narrator he is merely following Bledsoe's instructions. But in actuality, the system has all along been controlled by the older Emersons of the world. The frontier spirit that guided this country in its earliest days was self-reliance. The insistence on freedom from England and other European nations was based on self-reliance. The institution of slavery was the means whereby some might gain greater self-reliance at the price of other people's freedom. Self-reliance has, in some form or another, been with us from America's inception though it of course has not been beneficial to everyone.

Young Emerson claims to want to help our narrator, but the job he first offers is that of being a valet. It is only after the narrator declines this position that Emerson then suggests Liberty Paints which, with its slogan "If It's Optic White, It's the Right White," discriminates against black employees and even relegates one black to a post in the basement. Ellison has so cleverly concealed the essence of Brockway that we do not know if he is meant to be the Devil or if he is meant to personify the methods that blacks throughout history have used to survive in society.

Brockway, having begun as a maintenance man, has acquired the skills of an engineer, mastering the company's complex machinery. His place is still in the basement, but the company cannot function without him.

In "What America Would Be Like Without Blacks," Ellison points to the phenomenon of whites seizing "upon the presence of black Americans and [using] them as a marker, a symbol of limits, a metaphor for the 'outsider.'"[32] The artist believed that the reason whites can be white (with all the accompanying social advantages) is because blacks are black. One group's identity depends on the other. Whites may hold the position of dominance, but it is the very fact of blackness that enables that dominance to persist. Brockway lets us know that he was the one who helped the company president create the corporate slogan. And for that deed he received a $300 bonus, a reward given in essence for the act of appearing to know his place. He looms as a prime example of what it took for a black man in the 1930s to survive in the corporate world.

Brockway tells the narrator, "Usually they sends down some young white fellow who thinks he's going to watch me a few days and ask me a heap of questions and then take over."[33] Employment discrimination has been a feature of our society from the time of slavery when blacks were forced to work for free and then given no credit even when they conceived ingenious inventions. As time passed and industrialization led to the proliferation of large corporations, blacks were occasionally hired, but were subjected to severe restrictions. Liberty Paints' white management team sends its promising white trainees down to Brockway for corporate development. His job is to train them so that they can more effectively supervise him and perhaps eventually even make his job obsolete. The fact that Brockway has been able to withstand this occupational assault for so long makes him a hero in the truest sense of black survivalist folkloric tradition.

That janitor opposes the efforts of other blacks at the company who seek to form a workers' union; he and the narrator actually descend to the level of a fist fight over this issue. The narrator does not comprehend the nuances of Brockway's situation or the subtleties of any black man's situation in a white-owned company. But as he looks at the goo on Brockway's overalls, he thinks of Tar Baby without realizing exactly what the folklore character's connection is to the elderly black man with whom he is now confronted. In Joel Chandler Harris's version of the Tar Baby story, Brer Rabbit is curious about the tarred figure, not knowing that Brer Fox has set it out as a trap. Brer Rabbit gets stuck and Brer Fox has his mind set on making a meal of the smaller animal. As the fox prepares to skin him alive, the rabbit issues a response that is reminiscent of the invisible man's grandfather who ordered his progeny, "Live with your head in the lion's mouth."[34] In Harris's tale, as the rabbit is about to be skinned, he urges the fox onward, "Skin me ... snatch out my eyeballs, t'ar out my years by de roots, en cut off my legs."[35] Now the fox has to be thinking that something is wrong. He wants to hurt the rabbit as much as possible. But if the fox does what the rabbit wants, it certainly cannot be the absolute worst punishment. Logic demands that the fox do what the rabbit most abhors. The rabbit is begging him, "Please ... don't fling me in dat brier-patch," and the fox responds by doing exactly what the rabbit says he does not want; the fox flings him into the brier patch, and the rabbit, at home in the brier patch, happily scoots off to freedom.

Though he has goo on his overalls, Brockway does not signify Tar Baby. He is instead a version of Brer Rabbit. He has been "in the lion's mouth," so to speak, and tussled with adversity to the point where he is now covered with the sticky tar substance. In "Hidden Name and Complex Fate," Ellison urges us to

> let Tar Baby ... stand for the world. He leans, black and gleaming, against the wall of life utterly noncommittal under our scrutiny.... we touch him playfully and before we can say *Sonny Liston!* we find ourselves stuck. Our playful investigations become a labor, an *agon*. Slowly we perceive that our task is to learn the proper way of freeing ourselves to develop, in other words, technique.[36]

This is the lesson that *Invisible Man*'s narrator must learn. As he ponders what young Emerson's ulterior motive might be, he asks the vital question, "Who was I anyway?" Commenting further in the "Hidden Name and Complex Fate" essay, Ellison asserts that the enigmatic Tar Baby has many names, "all spelling chaos." But before we can know even one of those names, in hopes of eliminating the chaos and absurdity, we must set ourselves to the task of learning exactly who we are, "come into the possession of our own names."

Surely the narrator has a name. In fact the Brotherhood organization, of which he becomes a member, takes away his real name and substitutes another. We as readers, however, never know that name, which makes us question the notion of individuality, especially as we hear organization members such as Brother MacAfee declaring that "none of us as individuals count." One assumption rather common among literary critics is that the Brotherhood symbolizes the Communist Party. The Communist Party of America certainly had a large following in the 1930s, fueled in large part by the widespread disillusionment caused by the Great Depression. But in actuality the Brotherhood could symbolize any organization which has, as its chief aim, survival of the organization even to the extent of sacrificing the individuality of its members.

Such was Ellison's concern also with institutions of higher learning. As we hear the Reverend Homer Barbee praising the virtues of the Founder, we can be relatively certain that Ellison was using the model of his own alma mater — Tuskegee Institute — for his fictional portrayal of the southern black college, Booker T. Washington being the quintessential black college president who had to build an educational institution out of practically nothing, surrounded all the while by whites intent on perpetuating a second-class citizenship status for the black race. In the midst of such vehement opposition, how did those early black presidents function? How did they succeed in their goals?

I am always intrigued when I pick up Washington's autobiographical *Up from Slavery*, and read where he says that "at the top of the list" of his favorite audiences were northern businessmen. Now, being from the South myself and having visited numerous small southern towns, I can say with authority that during his lifetime, Washington was revered by southern blacks in a manner not unlike what might be reserved for a god. Why would the orator not specify that audience as one of his favorites? Upon analyzing the following autobiographical statement, we get a further sense of that college president's cunning:

> The time will come when the Negro in the South will be accorded all the political rights which his ability, character, and material possessions entitle him to. I think, though, that the opportunity to freely exercise such political rights will not come in any large degree through outside or artificial forcing, but will be accorded to the Negro by the Southern white people themselves, and that they will protect him in the exercise of those rights.[37]

Though we cannot know for sure what Washington meant exactly with his reference to rights based on "ability, character, and material possessions," it is useful to examine Ellison's Bledsoe who at one point "composed his angry face like a sculptor, making it a bland mask."[38] We are witness to the art of deception. Recall Paul Laurence Dunbar's poem "We Wear the Mask" with its poignant explanation of why African Americans throughout history have had to keep their true feelings in check.[39] "Did you forget how to lie?" Bledsoe scolded the invisible man. "Live with your head in the lion's mouth," his grandfather demanded, "Our life is a war." The narrator's head was often left spinning, trying to fathom what it all meant.

In his sermon before the college students, Barbee lauds the deceased Founder as a "prophet.... slave born, but marked from the beginning by a high intelligence and princely personality; born in the lowest part of this barren, war-scarred land, yet somehow shedding light upon it where'er he passed through."[40] The preacher has reference to the post–Civil War period which in some respects was even more torturous than slavery. Blacks were now legally free, but in which direction should they proceed in a society where legal freedom did not eliminate societal "shackles." According to Barbee, it was men such as the Founder and Bledsoe who would chart the appropriate course. He is "worthy of your imitation," the reverend insists. But then we learn that Barbee is physically blind, unable himself to determine direction and, on a symbolic level, unable to ascertain a suitable moral leadership.

Was the Founder a prophet providing "light"? In describing his alma mater, Ellison's narrator reflects on the "bronze statue" that seems to be but a fictional version of the memorial to Booker T. Washington that exists on the grounds of Tuskegee University. The statue is symbolic of a crucial ambiguity as the narrator tells us

> in my mind's eye I see the bronze statue of the college Founder, the cold Father symbol, his hands outstretched in the breathtaking gesture of lifting a veil that flutters in hard, metallic folds above the face of a kneeling slave; and I am standing puzzled, unable to decide whether the veil is really being lifted, or lowered more firmly in place; whether I am witnessing a revelation or a more efficient blinding.[41]

As the narrator thus reflects, we question the extent to which Washington may or may not have been primarily concerned with the best interests of blacks. Washington's contemporary, W. E. B. Du Bois, criticized how "Mr. Washington represents in Negro thought the old attitude of adjustment and submission."[42] It was Du Bois's belief that Washington was willing to sacrifice civil rights and even black higher education for his own accumulation of power. It was in 1881, less than two decades after slavery had ended, that Washington opened what was then called the Tuskegee Normal School for Colored Youth. There in the deep South, he initiated what would later become one of America's more prominent educational institutions. Nevermind that de facto slavery still existed, or that the Ku Klux Klan dominated southern politics, or that whites in general still regarded blacks as little more than beasts of burden. In the midst of all that, Washington laid the foundation for what would become one of America's most famous historically black universities.

What path did he pursue for this achievement even as he lived with his "head in the lion's mouth," building a college surrounded by viperous racism. History occasionally labels him an accommodationist. But then again, is not that how the world viewed our narrator's grandfather, a meek, "quiet old man" who "give up [his] gun back in the Reconstruction" when in actuality he was a "spy in the enemy's country." This is the ambiguity with which we must regard the grandfather's life as well as Washington's. And our narrator must forge an identity for himself even as he contemplates the emotionally brutal course that those two black men before him had trekked.

Du Bois understood the trickery involved when Washington, in his 1895 Atlanta Exposition speech, declared to a racially mixed audience, "In all things that are purely social we can be as separate as the fingers, yet one as the hand in all things essential to mutual progress."[43] It was an ingenious metaphor, this hand that, for blacks, symbolized racial equality while, for whites, it symbolized a continuation of staunch segregationist policy. But in spite of understanding the ploy, Du Bois still regarded the college president's tactics as detrimental to black social progress.

By way of contrast, steel magnate Andrew Carnegie gave a speech in Edinburgh, Scotland in 1907, calling Booker T. Washington

> the combined Moses and Joshua of his people.... one of those extraordinary men who rise at rare intervals and work miracles ... a modest gentlemanly man, of pure simple life and engaging qualities, supremely wise ... certainly one of the most wonderful men living or who has ever lived.[44]

And that view was typical of how northern industrialists perceived the Tuskegee president. Prominent white southerners were also inclined to praise him in terms that were ordinarily reserved for distinguished white southerners such as Robert E. Lee and Jefferson Davis. Washington's stature became so great in fact that during the first decade of the 20th century, President Theodore Roosevelt regularly solicited his advice on significant matters including presidential appointments.

The college president of Ellison's novel demands of our narrator to "learn where you are and get yourself power, influence, contacts with powerful and influential people — then stay in the dark and use it!"[45] As one can assume Washington had to do from time to time, Bledsoe admits, "Yes, I had to act the nigger!" He was forced to play the role that whites expected of him. It was the role that our narrator had unwittingly played at the battle royal when he changed "social equality" to "social responsibility," upon the demand of his white controllers. Now Bledsoe is telling him that the world will not change, "there's nothing else to do." This "acting the nigger" is a role that blacks have had to play from the beginnings of slavery on up to the present. Bledsoe, like Washington himself, is the quintessential trickster who survives and prospers only to the extent that he is able to hide his true convictions.

Young Emerson asks the narrator to "throw off the mask of custom." But such a request is inappropriate, for how can the black man be certain that he will survive if he lays bare his feelings before prominent whites who hold the power of life and death over him? Absent racial equality, there can be no mutuality of trust.

It is to Emerson's credit that he reconsiders and retracts his request. "Frankness just isn't possible," he laments, "because all our motives are impure."[46] Ralph Waldo Emerson, in "Self-Reliance," criticizes philanthropy because it lessens the independence of the recipient of the largesse. But beyond that, the philosopher considered so-called "good works" to be in actuality apologies for "living in the world," and far from fostering self-reliance, perpetual gift giving renders the recipient a subservient debtor to the benefactor who now can feel justified in pursuing his primary life's objective.

Critic Leonard Deutsch observes that by contributing to Bledsoe's college, Mr. Norton is "buying off his conscience" at the same time that he expects a "profitable return on his investment." Deutsch further elucidates that "when the paternalistic Norton advocates 'self-reliance' to the black students he means acquiring a trade so that the Negroes can compete with the white man in the commercial world (and so, incidentally, reduce the wages Mr. Norton must pay his employees)."[47] It has been the case over the generations that the boards of trustees of historically black colleges have primarily consisted of wealthy, influential whites who, one must imagine, have had agendas that did not always coincide with the best interests of the black college students to whom money was given. Norton tells our narrator, "You are my fate," as if both their lives are wonderfully intertwined in a glorious march down the road toward racial progress. In actuality, the northern philanthropist knows very little about the black college students whose best interests he purports to have at heart. The narrator is for Norton just what one of the vets at the Golden Day says: "invisible, a walking personification of the Negative, the most perfect achievement of your dreams, sir! The mechanical man."[48] The narrator, at this point in the novel, has such faith in Norton that this philanthropist becomes not so much a man anymore but "a God, a force." Meanwhile for Norton, the narrator never was a man or even a human being so much as he is a prospective cog in the machinery of a developing industrialization.

Young Emerson, in spite of the help that he offers the invisible man, changes nothing about the basic nature of things. He is as much interested in having sex with the narrator as in anything else. And it is through this sort of basic sexual urge that Ellison seeks to universalize a reality of human existence. The wealthy white Norton can identify with the black sharecropper Trueblood because they both have incestuous feelings for their daughters. The "leading white citizens" who stage the battle royal are sexually aroused at the sight of black boys in the presence of a naked white woman. And even a wise vet is not free from the turmoil of race-driven sexuality as he tells the narrator that once he gets to New York, he "might even dance with a white girl."

In *Sex and Racism in America*, sociologist Calvin Hernton portrays society as an "intricate network of social, political, economic, and moral evils that make it impossible for any American — black or white — to grow up fully sane."[49] That author acknowledges that sexual ills have had as devastating an impact upon the American psyche as the stratification of individuals into racial and social classes. In such a world, what are the odds that our narrator will come into a knowledge of himself whereby he can make consistent contributions to the general society? For if he does not say what he is told and act in accordance with social expectations, his fate may be even worse than the place where he resides at the end of the novel. In that underground dwelling, he has reconciled himself with his condition of invisibility and is safe, for the time, from those forces who would exploit him for their various purposes. But he is also severely restricted, no longer a participant in the battle raging just beyond his solitary well-lit den.

"What Shall a Man Give in Exchange for His Soul?": Gloria Naylor's Persistent Query

During the late 1960s, Gloria Naylor traveled throughout the South as a Protestant preacher, so it is not all that surprising that she would be concerned in her novels with the symbolic portent of people compelled to sell, in the metaphorical sense, their souls for one reason or another. In Matthew 16:26, Jesus asks the pertinent question, "What is a man profited, if he shall gain the whole world, and lose his own soul? or what shall a man give in exchange for his soul?" Jesus' specific concern was with how so many people are intent on accumulating wealth at practically any cost, including to the point where morality is altogether sacrificed.

The evil, as Naylor presents it, has to do with the phenomenon of some African Americans rejecting their heritage in the effort to fit into both the predominantly white corporate world and the American mainstream in general. No character in Naylor's novels epitomizes the social and psychological trade-off as much as Linden Hills's Maxwell Smyth with his silk scarves, tweed jackets, Dartmouth degree, and assortment of other materialistic accouterments. Moreover, he is so mechanical in his actions that he must turn his Stingray ignition off with an exact "forty-five-degree turn of his wrist," and then he always waits "exactly three seconds" before he pulls out the key. As Naylor puts it, "His entire life became a race against the natural — and he was winning."[1] The full extent of the process becomes all the more clear as we learn that he has been so successful at rejecting the natural in himself that he no longer has a need for toilet paper. His diet consists of vegetables, juices, baby scallops, calves' liver, and breasts of squab in addition to the spring water and chamomile tea with which he "purifies" his system to the point where when he does go to the toilet at the exact moment each day, he eliminates a substance that bears no resemblance to ordinary human waste.

Why does he go to all this trouble? What does he hope to achieve? One might conclude that in pursuing this particular digestive process, he hopes to achieve long life. But something else is in operation here. Something having to do with gaining acceptance into the more exclusive realms of white society. At Dartmouth he had been "always immaculate and controlled." And then upon graduation, he rapidly advanced through the ranks at General Motors, rising from regional sales representative to assistant to the executive director. Indeed, Smyth has expectations of one day taking over as executive director of this major corporation. It is at least to his credit that he does understand how his life has become a virtual "tightrope" walk where, as he tells Xavier Donnell, "the rope's a lot thinner than you think and it's a lot farther to the ground."[2]

Donnell, the vice-president for Minority Marketing at GM, feels fortunate that Smyth has taken him under his wing. "They were," Naylor tells us, "the only two black men on the tenth floor at GM, and Maxwell's office was even closer to the executive director's than his."[3] These two black men can work together on strategies for survival in a "world" that was once alien to them but now one where they are finding themselves beginning to belong. Writing in 1982 for *The New York Times Magazine*, Bebe Moore Campbell assessed the "first generation" of black corporate managers and described the delicacy of their situation:

> Isolated from other blacks and alienated from whites, [they] straddle two worlds. They consciously choose their speech, their walk, their mode of dress and car; they trim their hair lest a mountainous Afro set them apart. They know they have a high visibility, and realize that their success depends not only on their abilities, but also on their white colleagues feeling comfortable with them.[4]

In *Black Life in Corporate America: Swimming in the Mainstream*, a book published the same year that Campbell made her pronouncements, George Davis and Glegg Watson presented the perspectives of various black managers working in predominantly white corporations. One of the managers interviewed in that study declared with a sense of resignation:

> They want you to be like them.... They want you to suppress certain aspects of your racial identity — your life-style, sense of humor, way

of dressing — existential things that are part of your racial heritage. I can do it. I can "behave." "Behave" means act the way they want you to.[5]

What Campbell, Davis, and Watson were addressing was the "tightrope" phenomenon to which Naylor's Smyth refers, a tenuousness that consists of blacks in certain positions having to watch their every move, measure every step for white acceptability in hopes that they might be able to rise up the corporate ladder. Don't get me wrong. Whites, particularly white women in middle- and upper-management positions, also have to play a rigorous game of office politics in order to prove their acceptability. But blacks have been scrutinized even more in the high-stakes game of corporate advancement.

Smyth is consumed by this process, living with his guard up virtually each waking moment of his life. He "weighed the decision of whether or not to smile at his secretary with the same gravity as that with which he considered the advisability of a new line of sedans."[6] We know of his bathroom habits at home. But even at work, he is a specialist in "latrine politics," with a control over his bowels so precise that nothing has to be eliminated until he decides "where and how much." A worthy mentor, one might assume, for Donnell who cannot even decide whether it is strategically appropriate to marry the woman with whom he has fallen in love.

The woman is Roxanne Tilson who, on the surface at least, seems an excellent choice for an upwardly mobile black man of Donnell's professional caliber. With her B.A. from Wellesley and ad agency job, one would think she would be a worthy complement as he negotiates his climb up the corporate ladder. Naylor informs us that "her life consisted of nibbles." And sure enough, her eating habits are reminiscent of Smyth's delicate cuisine. Tilson tries to stick to a diet of cottage cheese, "dabs" of fish, and "bits" of lettuce and cucumber. But unlike Smyth, she falls into periods of despair and turns for solace to potato chips, French chocolates, and Hostess Twinkies. So her body is fully curved, giving "the impression that it was just one good meal away from being labeled fat."[7]

And this, Smyth sees as a serious problem. It is bad enough, from the mentor's perspective, that she lives at the *top* of Linden Hills, not in one of the more prestigious houses lower down. But added to that is the prospect that she will get fat. Smyth warns his protégé:

> Most black women have a tendency to let themselves go. Look in
> any spa or gym and they're outnumbered ten to one.... it's not Rox-
> anne's fault. It's an old throwback to the jungle days when they had
> to store up food like camels because the women did most of the
> hauling. So what they do now is starve themselves until they get you
> and then gain ten pounds before the reception's over.[8]

It is somewhat amazing that a man of Smyth's intellect can be so sus-
ceptible to the prevailing racial stereotypes. In characterizing how
Tilson will look in the future as a "throwback to the jungle days," his
abounding self-hatred is evident. For him, certain blacks are still "pick-
aninnies," "jungle bunnies," niggers. But perhaps we should not be all
that surprised. After all, this is the same man who "spent every waking
moment trying to be no color at all."[9] He "seemed to have made the very
elements disappear, while it was no more than the psychological sleight-
of-hand that he used to make his blackness disappear."[10]

He criticizes black women, many of whom indeed have a tendency
to gain weight in the hip area. But he, on the other hand, is not critical of white women, many of whom have a tendency to accumulate
wrinkles that make them look old beyond their years. He is not critical
of white women because he has adopted the attitudes of the dominant
culture. But even more generally, whatever the race of the woman, she
can never be anything more than an ornament, an asset to be held or
bartered away depending on what he perceives at any given moment as
her ultimate value in the pursuit of his professional goal.

Such a perspective is one upon which the Linden Hills community
was founded. Rumor has it that the first Luther Nedeed actually sold his
octoroon wife and his children for money he then used to buy the property upon which the Linden Hills houses were built. Then he returned
to Mississippi and brought back an even younger octoroon wife to begin
a new process of childbearing. As Naylor's novel begins, there have been
five generations of Luther Nedeeds with their light-skinned wives who
personify white culture by virtue of their skin color. And yet, each of
those women learn what Tilson soon discovers, that all the hair relaxers and bleaching creams in the world will not garner them respect as
human beings. By the time we arrive at the current Linden Hills generation, we find Donnell (heeding his mentor Smyth's advice) opting
to date white women exclusively.

Another example of erroneous advising presents itself in the situation of the homosexual black lawyer Winston Alcott. Once again, the

issue concerns who is an appropriate mate for someone who is scaling the corporate ladder. Alcott, a young lawyer in the firm of Farragut and Conway, is persuaded by his father to marry a woman for the sake of appearances. "Remember who you are," the father demands, "A law firm like Farragut and Conway would kick you out tomorrow if you sneezed wrong."[11] It is of course ironic that the father here is appealing to the notion of self-knowledge when, for his son, being true to himself would demand that he follow his homosexual instincts. But the father has reference to a different identity, the one that is imbedded in the culture of social hierarchy epitomized by Linden Hills.

And the "keeper" of Linden Hills, Nedeed himself, is the one who drives the limousine that escorts Alcott and two others in the wedding entourage. Not coincidentally, it is the same limousine that takes corpses to their resting place at the bottom of the community. As Alcott denies his essential self for financial prosperity, he takes a step further down in the direction where Nedeed can claim his soul as he has claimed so many others. It was Nedeed who sent the anonymous letter to Alcott's father, threatening to expose the son's sexual orientation to the senior partner at the law firm. Having examined, in the previous chapter, the situations of Clarence Cain and Ellison's young Emerson, we know what the repercussions of public disclosure can be, destroying both the career and the person himself who has been tagged with the homosexual label.

Critic Margaret Homans characterizes Linden Hills as "a machine for turning out phantoms, with Nedeed turning the crank.... [He] provokes and then silently observes one suicide, and arranges the soul-destroying marriage of a homosexual man whom he knows will end as another suicide."[12] The soul-destroying marriage to which Homans refers is indeed the one between Alcott and a nondescript woman we know only as Cassandra. We can assume, however, that she is very much like Roxanne Tilson and the generations of Nedeed wives who were so intent on marriage to an upwardly mobile black man that they did not stop to consider what marriage without love would be like. And Alcott himself will similarly be left unfulfilled since it is not Cassandra but his lover David who "gave him his center." Still, Alcott is able to deny David and issue the ultimatum, "I can't live with you. Not in Linden Hills. That would be suicide, and you know it."[13] Alcott is referring here to career suicide. But Homans is correct; as Alcott proceeds with the formality of a meaningless marriage, he is also moving further in the direction of a literal suicide that will be the final rendering of his soul to Nedeed ergo the Devil.

The other suicide to which Homans refers is the one committed by Laurel Dumont who earlier in her life had woven a brilliant tapestry of personal freedom through her love of music and swimming. As she explains to her grandmother Roberta Johnson,

> It's all in the balance and how you hit the surface. And it's the greatest feeling in the world when you do it right, Grandma. It's like there's no difference between the air and the water except that the water is safer. Once you get down there and hold still, it lifts you right up, sorta like it was a pair of warm hands or arms. And you come up to all this beautiful music that was really there anyway if you knew how to listen.[14]

We can readily observe that Dumont, as a child, was one with the natural elements. And indeed it was her summer trips to Georgia, where her grandmother lived, that facilitated the spiritual development. But then something happened that is perhaps comparable to what happened to Smyth during his college days at Dartmouth. All Grandma Johnson knows is "that she had cashed in her life insurance to send a child … to the state of California, and it sent her back a stranger."[15] Dumont attended the University of California at Berkeley where one must imagine her priority changed from the search for self-fulfillment to a need to enter the corporate world and locate the appropriate husband. She found Howard Dumont whose family had owned their Linden Hills home for the past 60 years but, as Naylor specifies, they "could boast of nothing but the sweaty backs of lawyers on their sheets and the grime of government officials swirling down their drains."[16] Howard continued in the family tradition by becoming a district attorney in Wayne County. Laurel, on the other hand, even with her career at IBM (indeed she has become the "biggest woman" at IBM), is beginning to understand that something is tragically wrong.

It was the sociologist E. Franklin Frazier who, writing with great foresight in 1957, noted

> one of the most important consequences of the emergence of the black bourgeoisie, namely, the uprooting of this stratum of the Negro population from its "racial" traditions or, more specifically, from its folk background. As the result of the break with its cultural past, the black bourgeoisie is without cultural roots in either the Negro world with which it refuses to identify, or the white world which refuses to permit the black bourgeoisie to share its life.[17]

What Frazier was portraying was the no-man's land that existed between two distinct cultures, one white and the other black with its origins going all the way back to slavery. It is this latter culture that Howard, his family, and others like him have denied. Such perhaps is the price of success. But as they lose the essence of who they are, exactly where then do they belong?

Laurel hastens back to Georgia in the effort to retrieve the deeper meanings of her life, but her grandmother conveys the mystical puzzling message that "Georgia wasn't really home for you. It was just a shack where you had learned to be at home with yourself.... If you feel you've lost that, Laurel, you didn't lose it in Georgia and so there weren't no point in coming back there trying to find it."[18] Where did Laurel lose it? Berkeley? That would be the simple response. But the process of losing herself actually began earlier, down in Georgia. Grandma Johnson used to tell Brer Fox and Brer Bear stories to Laurel, much to that granddaughter's delight. But after a point, the grandmother "didn't get the smile she was used to." It is important to consider that just as Laurel is ceasing to get as much enjoyment from the Brer Fox and Brer Bear stories, the grandmother is planning to "put one of them new relaxers" in her granddaughter's hair. Even if the grandmother is meant to personify a rich African American culture, she cannot prevent the infiltration of white mainstream values. So it is not Georgia per se where Laurel lost her identity. Nor did she lose it in one fell swoop at Berkeley. Rather, the nature of Laurel's victimization has to do with the existence of an intrinsically American process where the choice becomes one of assimilating or suffering the consequences of alienation.

Still struggling to recreate her lost childhood, Laurel converts her Linden Hills den into a music room and has the garage moved and backyard excavated so that she can install a swimming pool. But such strategies fall short of achieving her ultimate desire. Notice how she has only changed those parts of her home that are auxiliary — the den, the garage, the backyard. The core parts of the house remain intact. Moreover, it had never been just the location where she played music that was all that important. Nor was it merely a concrete pool that had given her essence in the past. Instead, it had been her *perspective* on the music and swimming that had provided her with her identity. As her perspective on those activities changed, the building of a new music room and a new swimming pool are but shallow reminders of a soul irretrievably lost.

As might be expected, Nedeed appears on the scene at a crucial juncture demanding that she vacate the premises. And here is where we see how important it is, from her perspective, that she hold on to whatever vestige she can of her upper-middle-class lifestyle. When Nedeed informs her that the 1000-year lease agreement between his family and Howard's has been broken, she rails back that "Howard speaks for Howard, and I speak for me.... And I have as much say about the future of this property as he does."[z] But the lease agreements in Linden Hills are based on a patriarchal system that gives decision-making power to the husband. She is separated from her husband and there are no children to inherit the lease, so she legally has no option but to leave. And considering her already desperate need for some emotional solace, she is no match for Nedeed in pursuit of his ultimate objective. He knows the lengths to which she has been driven and watches with delight from his place in the shadows as she dives headlong from the 30-foot-high diving board into the empty swimming pool.

Kiswana Browne in *The Women of Brewster Place* might have met with a similar fate had she not decided to flee Linden Hills and move to the Brewster Place housing project. Having changed her name from "Melanie," she perceives her life's mission to include living among the less fortunate of the black race, where she can offer direct assistance. And it can be argued that the aim has been largely achieved, particularly with her organization of a tenants association and the staging of Shakespeare's *A Midsummer Night's Dream*.

An important question, however, concerns whether or not her upbringing in Linden Hills has been such an influencing factor in her life that, even with her attempts to reclaim a distinct African American heritage, mainstream American values still rise to the surface. For example, why does Browne stage a Shakespearean play instead of one written by a black playwright? And at the all-important block party that concludes the novel, one ponders whether, in spite of her presence there, she still does not fully belong. At one point when a group of Brewster Place women laugh heartily at a joke, she is unable to join in the laughter, being more inclined herself to analyze the joke's content. And what should we make of the fact that she is primarily fearful of the coming rain that will serve as a baptism at the party? "We better start clearing up," she urges. If she had her way, the "dream" segment of the novel might never have occurred in the way that it did with the revitalizing rain serving as a symbol for black sisterhood.

Furthermore, it is essential that the women are trying to tear down the wall that had separated them from the rest of the city. Yet Browne is "staring at the wall, as if trying to remember something important that had escaped her."[20] A Brewster Place resident was raped at this wall. That Browne, even for a second, cannot recall its significance is Naylor's way of telling us that there is still a considerable psychological distance between this character and those other women who now understand how the wall had been a device for their imprisonment.

Perhaps the critic Barbara Christian expresses it best as she elaborates on the distinction between Browne and other Brewster Place women:

> She can leave Brewster Place when she wishes. She does not risk survival, as the others would if they rebelled; nor has she yet been worn down by the unceasing cycle of displacement that the others have experienced.... Naylor's inclusion of Kiswana ... indicates the great distance between women who *must* live in women-centered communities and those who have the option to live in them.[21]

However much Browne wants to identify with the plights of Brewster Place women, she still has access to privileges characteristic of those who live in Linden Hills. In fact, though the "Kiswana Browne" chapter appears on the surface to be a study in contrast between her and her mother (Mrs. Browne), it is the similarities between the two women that eventually come to the fore. In telling the story of her own mother, Mrs. Browne depicts her as a woman "who bore nine children and educated them all, who held off six white men with a shotgun when they tried to drag one of her sons to jail for 'not knowing his place.'"[22] Mrs. Browne gave her daughter the name "Melanie" as a tribute to that woman and to provide her with a sense of pride and dignity. It is ironic that the daughter would later change her name to "Kiswana" for the very same reason.

The daughter Browne dropped out of college so that she could "be in the streets with [her] people." She wanted to have more of an impact on the lives of housing project residents than merely being in college would allow. Mrs. Browne understands this, but she thinks her daughter might have been able to do more had she first completed college and then gone into politics or opened a "school in this very neighborhood." As the chapter closes, we learn that both mother and daughter have perhaps chosen the same type of mate, men who love them from the tips of their heads down to the soles of their feet. Browne realizes

> that her mother had trod through the same universe that she herself was now traveling. Kiswana was breaking no new trails and would

eventually end up just two feet away on that couch. She
stared at the woman she had been and was to become.[23]

Mother and daughter are of the same spirit. And in the very last para-
graph of the "Kiswana Browne" chapter, we have the starkest evidence
of that to which Christian refers in making the distinction between
Kiswana Browne and the women "who *must* live" in Brewster Place.
Before leaving, Mrs. Browne had slipped $75 in between the cushions
of her daughter's sofa. The daughter could have given the money back.
Indeed as the chapter closes, we find her at the window, about to yell
down to her mother "who had just emerged from the building." But the
daughter changes her mind and sinks "in the chair with a long sigh that
caught in the upward draft of the autumn wind and disappeared over
the top of the building."[24] The operative words there are "sigh" and "disappeared." The exasperation she had felt upon discovering the money
has now changed to relief at being able to receive this financial support.

In spite of those difficulties in assessing Browne, she still is not as
problematic as her brother Wilson who in college never took part in
social protests and "even refused to wear an Afro." During the 1960s and
early 1970s, there was much for the typical college student to be alarmed
about, from civil rights issues to Vietnam to insufficient numbers of
black faculty and black students. It says a great deal about Wilson, as a
person, that he could stand by and watch apathetically while others
became immersed in those crucial battles.

The reason it is so important to consider the significance of long
hair (as it was worn during the late 1960s and early 1970s) is due to the
symbolic portent of it as a statement itself of discontent with the estab-
lishment, the status quo. And for blacks who wore the long Afro hairstyles during that era, it was even more profoundly a refusal of capitulation to mainstream values. Wilson, by not growing an Afro, was
making a different statement that consisted of his willingness to do
whatever it took to get a job and be accepted by that mainstream culture. We will recall it was Bebe Campbell who characterized the first
generation of black corporate managers as a group who had to "trim
their hair lest a mountainous Afro set them apart." Wilson's conformity
is a testament to what has been perceived by some as the necessity of
that particular self-negational act.

After his college years Wilson obtains employment, and his mother
praises how he has found a job and is "settled with a family." But her
use of the word "settled" is rather troublesome. Our analyses of the

characters Donnell and Alcott in *Linden Hills* revealed how dissatisfying it can be to marry solely in response to societal expectations. And it isn't just marriage for conformity that can be the source of dissatisfaction. Biff Loman, in Arthur Miller's *Death of a Salesman*, ponders the reasons why he might be unhappy and thinks maybe he "oughta get married." Then he considers that perhaps it is not marriage after all that he needs, and so he asks his bachelor brother Happy, "Are you content?" to which Happy responds:

> I don't know what the hell I'm workin' for. Sometimes I sit in my apartment — all alone.... And it's crazy. But then, it's what I always wanted. My own apartment, a car, and plenty of women. And still, goddammit, I'm lonely.[25]

It was Grandma Roberta in *Linden Hills* who remarked, "I guess what folks say is true then. It's lonely at the top."[26] Her granddaughter Laurel had replied, "It's damned lonely." Both Laurel and Happy are frustrated in spite of their corporate positions. Mere social status, as is the case with marriage, is not enough in the final analysis for personal fulfillment.

The plight of Browne's brother would seem to be not all that different from Laurel and Happy's. When Mrs. Browne praises him for having a good job, Kiswana replies scornfully, "He's an assistant to an assistant junior partner in a law firm."[27] What exactly does that job title mean? We learn from Mrs. Browne's comments that Wilson finished college and then "went on for his law degree." Should we assume that he finished law school? Yet, the entry level position at law firms is "associate," associate to the partners. Once an associate becomes a partner himself, then he may be a junior partner. But what does "assistant junior partner" mean? Such a title would be strange enough, but even stranger is Browne's actual characterization of her brother as an "assistant to an assistant junior partner." Perhaps that sister exaggerates. Or maybe it is incorrect to assume that the brother completed his law school requirements, passed the bar examination, and joined the law firm at the typical entry-level position. What we can be reasonably sure of, however, is that Naylor wants us to regard his position at the firm as incongruous with what should be an ultimately satisfying employment situation.

In *The Rage of a Privileged Class*, Ellis Cose examines the circumstances of blacks working in predominantly white law firms and concludes that "if in fact blacks tend to be tracked into certain areas, and if in fact blacks are therefore destined to progress more slowly than whites, and if in fact the real reasons for advancement have less to do with ability than with attributes one is *a priori* assumed to possess, then it is only to be expected, given certain widespread racial assumption in America, that very few blacks, however accomplished, manage to get near the top of the corporate hierarchy."[28] Cose further notes that as late as 1974, the approximate time that Wilson would have been entering the job market, there were only three black partners in major New York law firms. Discrimination on the basis of race is the only possible explanation for such a deplorable statistic.

Kiswana labels her brother an "assistant to an assistant junior partner," and just as when Biff calls Happy an assistant to the assistant buyer, we should consider the job title's metaphorical significance. Rather than having found the pot at the end of a rainbow, what both Happy and Wilson have settled for is in actuality little more than the position of "glorified lackey." The task that those two men have ahead of them now involves justifying their position within the corporate structure to avoid their own emotional destruction.

That plight also sheds significant light on Winston Alcott in his quest to make full partner at the law firm where he works. He denies his sexual identity in the effort. But will it have been all for naught when the partners come to deciding whether or not he is "qualified" to be one of them. Upon reading *Why Should White Guys Have All the Fun?*, we learn that even TLC Beatrice International's Reginald Lewis had doubts that he could make partner at the New York City-based, white law firm where he was employed before he decided to go into business on his own.[29] If the case of Reginald Lewis is indicative of the general trend, then Cose is right on point as he outlines the various ways blacks are afforded less opportunity in the corporate setting. Cose further observes that "many whites get ahead in large part because they are beneficiaries of a congenial stereotype (which presupposes that executives and corporate lawyers are white), of early high-profile job assignments (which whites are more likely to get), of mentors (whom whites have an easier time acquiring)."[30] In other words, image becomes reality as even highly educated, performance-oriented blacks fall victim to the prevailing racial stereotypes.

I would be remiss if I did not consider here the issue of affirmative action. Has it helped or hurt in terms of how African Americans are perceived? Of course, there are those who regard affirmative action as the process whereby jobs are allotted to less-than-qualified blacks.

Many companies, on the other hand, benefit greatly by including minorities who in the past had been regularly excluded. A good example is the insurance industry. In a special report, *Newsweek*'s Peter Annin explained why this area of enterprise was eager to change: "Selling insurance in minority neighborhoods ... was a job particularly well suited to minorities, just as selling insurance in the suburbs was best done by hometown agents (whites) who knew their customers from Little League and the Lions Club."[31] Such a scenario would seem to provide increased opportunity for blacks, and in a certain sense it has. However, in assessing that "progress," it should not be ignored that firmly entrenched systems of racial segregation as yet remain unaltered.

Needless to say, it is always crucial to examine the reasons *why* blacks are hired and in what particular positions. Donnell is vice-president for minority marketing at GM. He holds this position for much the same reason that the insurance companies mentioned above began seeking out minority agents — to exploit a hitherto untapped profitable market. Just as in the case of newly hired black insurance agents, Donnell is a tool in the effort to corner a certain market. When his usefulness is ended, how will he be treated by superiors who no longer need this service? And Smyth's position as assistant to the executive director is no more guaranteed than Donnell's position in marketing. Smyth envisions himself one day becoming executive director. He assumes that "when the executive chair became vacant, the board of trustees wouldn't think twice about giving the best man the job. And that's the only kind of man he was."[32] The critic Margaret Homans declares of him that he is "the only character who is as much at home in Linden Hills as Nedeed."[33] He goes to extremes in altering his identity to fit in, to be accepted both by the company and the evil Nedeed. But it was Cose who was quick to remind us of the dearth of black CEOs in Fortune 500 companies. Smyth's rise to that level is highly improbable if indeed it is possible at all.

*   *   *

In Naylor's fourth novel, *Bailey's Cafe*, there is an intriguing section entitled "Miss Maple's Blues" that is the story of a black man (actually he has Mexican and Native American blood too) with the singular distinction of having received his Ph.D. in mathematics from Stanford University in the 1940s. Though his family is independently wealthy, he wants to achieve success on his own and declares:

> My goal was to open my own marketing firm. The first step was
> earning my own money. And you earn money by seeking employ-
> ment that you're qualified to perform. It was that simple. From Los
> Angeles to Philadelphia, I applied at firms and industrial corpora-
> tions that advertised for marketing analysts — no experience
> needed — and presented my credentials.[34]

Needless to say, he is more than qualified for the numerous "marketing
analyst" positions that are advertised in the newspapers. As he travels
across the country, he mails detailed proposals in advance, lines up
interviews, and then winds up being rejected as "they kept reading and
rereading my college transcripts, flipping through the charts…. and
then the shattered hopes when they finally looked back up at me and a
different man hadn't materialized in front of them."[35] His "A-" academic
average is not enough to overcome the handicap of his blackness. At one
company, he is offered the job of head custodian even though the position he had applied for was "statistical analyst." Continuing on, he
receives other offers for menial employment — bellboy, mailroom clerk,
elevator operator. But he continues his search for an analyst position.
His best offer (after 46 rejections for the research analyst position) is for
work as an assistant to the assistant foreman on an assembly line at an
automobile manufacturing plant in Detroit.

Now, considering my previous discussion about ploys on the part
of corporations to make blacks assistants instead of heads of overall
operations, we might be inclined to regard Maple's "assistant to the
assistant" job offer as just another example of the racial insult. Indeed
in Maple's case, the insult is just as evident as in the cases of Maxwell
Smyth, Xavier Donnell, and Wilson Browne. But it is apropos also to
consider the state of the automobile industry in the 1940s in order to
assess just what the black Stanford graduate is turning down. Describing what the conditions were at the Detroit automobile manufacturing
plants of that time, historians August Meier and Elliott Rudwick
describe how

> at Chrysler and Chevrolet blacks were employed as paint-sprayers;
> at another firm "certain dangerous emery steel grinding jobs were
> given only to Negroes." At Briggs, which had a particularly high
> proportion of heavy, unpleasant jobs, blacks were assigned princi-
> pally to the dirtiest and most disagreeable ones, notably in the Mack
> Avenue plant's paint-spray and wet-sanding department…. Pre-
> eminently, however, blacks labored at the hot and heavy work in the

foundries.... In General Motors, the Buick, Pontiac, and Chevrolet plants also concentrated blacks in the foundries; while GM's Fisher Body was lily-white except for the custodians. Even at Ford, black employees disproportionately held down the disagreeable jobs.[36]

Those circumstances would soon change to a certain extent, thanks in part to the efforts of the United Automobile Workers (UAW) union. But prior to that, blacks were generally relegated to the unskilled and semi-skilled jobs. We were more likely to be steel grinders, foundry workers, paint sprayers, and custodians; work that, as Meier and Rudwick attest, was both "disagreeable" and extremely dangerous.

As had been the case with the jobs of Wilson Browne in *Brewster Place* and Happy Loman in *Death of a Salesman*, one cannot say for certain, with regard to *Bailey's Cafe*, what "assistant to the assistant" actually means. In the latter work, that job description might simply be a glorified title for the type of labor that was typically performed by blacks during the early era of the automobile industry. Or perhaps the job offer is for work that is slightly or even substantially more agreeable than what was afforded blacks in general at the time. But if that is the case, why doesn't Maple accept this position as the best he can do at this point in time in American history?

The reason he does not accept it is because he is a man of deep principle. For a better understanding of his perspective on life, we must go back to the time when he was eighteen years old when he went to the freighting office with his father to pick up a 38-volume set of the works of William Shakespeare. The cover of each volume was "jet silk" with a "finely stitched" binding. The entire set was a gift from the father to the son as he was about to go off to college. But just outside the freighting office were the local bullies, the Gatlins, with their preconceived notions of blacks as inferior beings not worthy of simple respect.

It is apropos at this point also to assess the full name of the son, now Miss Maple, the then recipient of the Shakespeare collection. His previous name had been Stanley Beckwourth Booker T. Washington Carver. The father named him "Beckwourth" after the African American pioneer who discovered the easiest way for wagon trains to cross the Sierra Mountains. He named him "Booker T. Washington" after the Tuskegee Institute president, and "Carver" after the scientist who discovered over a hundred uses for the peanut. Stanley's father did not necessarily want his son to follow directly in the footsteps of those great men, but in so naming his child, he provided the basis both for pride in his heritage and for a means to see what he yet could accomplish regardless of the fact that he is a young black male.

The lesson that the father wanted to teach his son was made all the more difficult since Stanley, throughout his childhood, had absolutely no appreciation for his father's methods. Having speculated in land with a high success rate, the father then acquired a taste for fine clothes, but the son can only contemplate:

> I thought my father was pathetic for never fighting back. He had to know it wasn't accidental that a wad of tobacco spit would splatter right in front of us, staining the cuffs of his slacks. No storekeeper was so nearsighted that he waited on everyone else at the counter before he finally saw us. Holtville wasn't so crowded that we had to be bumped and shoved aside while trying to cross the street.[37]

Even today, it takes a great deal of patience to withstand the intentional insults accruing daily in the lives of African Americans. There are indeed those who would go utterly insane if they had to endure the perpetual indignities without recourse to lashing out at someone, anyone. Stanley, for his part, had more respect for his Uncle Leon who "once beat a man to a pulp just for calling him black."[38]

So when the Gatlins rip off the father's fine clothes, and Stanley's too for that matter, the son is incensed that his father will still not fight back. After they have been shoved into a storeroom, the father plots how they might slip out quietly, go to the authorities, and press charges. Stanley almost has to laugh at that latter proposition, knowing that justice for blacks was not to be found in America's courtrooms. They have almost stacked enough wooden crates to be able to climb out the back window when they realize that the Gatlins are urinating all over the Shakespeare volumes. This is when the father and son break out of the storeroom and take on the Gatlins in physical confrontation, breaking one's nose and another's rib until the last Gatlin left "was close to tears and started whining, Them others made me do it — I ain't wanted to. And I got a bad heart."[39] Witnessing the chain of events and noting how his father had "made his point," the son gains a newfound respect for the man whom he had previously regarded with utter contempt.

Recall the Gatlins had stripped off the clothes of Stanley and his father, all the while making crude remarks such as, "My God, look, it ain't got a tail after all.... And it ain't got a big wanger neither."[40] So what did the father and son wear when they burst through the door and took on the Gatlins? The father knew they had to wear something; he correctly surmised that the Gatlins would "go straight for the balls." In the storeroom was an unclaimed trunk marked "Lulu and the Little Ladies," containing dog costumes modeled after women's clothing. This is what the father put on and what he had his son wear also. And as Stanley tells us his story, he confirms how one Gatlin "did try to kick me in the balls. But his toe only kept making contact with the whalebone in front of my corset."[41] As strange as this outfit must have looked on Stanley, it nevertheless served the protective purpose that the father intended.

Years later, as he engages in his marathon interviewing schedule in search of a marketing analyst position, the thought occurs to Stanley that he should, at least on very hot days, change his dress attire. Upon scanning the bookshelves of my own local library, I have noticed that there are many "how to" books advising what a person should wear on a job interview. One of the more blatantly direct interpreters of corporate protocol with regard to this issue is John T. Molloy who devotes an entire book chapter to "Some Advice for Minorities." What he advises is that "if you are black or Spanish in America, and if you are moving up the rungs of corporate success, you should adhere to the dress code of the corporation and of the country, even going somewhat overboard in the direction of being conservative."[42] This is a rather common sense approach, I might add. We all know how important it is to "put your best foot forward," especially during the impressionable interview process.

Molloy's advice, albeit in some sense appropriate, nevertheless becomes rather frightening as he postulates that the "typical upper-middle-class American looks white." Anyone not possessing "his" characteristics, Molloy further contends, will "elicit a negative response in some degree." That expert further stipulates that the negative response can be conscious or subconscious. Interviewees and actual employees — who have been discriminated against due to race, dress, or some other aspect of their outward appearance — can suspect the cause for rejection, but if the "weeding out" process is mainly subconscious, how can it be declared with absolute certainty what the reason for rejection or dismissal was?

Blacks in America have been victimized by this process for time immemorial. Molloy, being practical, merely offers advice in terms of how one might circumvent prospective discrimination. And on days when it is cool, Stanley adheres to the corporate dress code, wearing his gray flannel suit with the vest. But on days when it is swelteringly hot, he opts to wear a woman's dress, flat sandals, sheer cotton stockings, and a straw bolero. This is what is comfortable. Thinking back to the episode in Holtville when he and his father burst out of the storeroom in the frilly costumes, the son now wears a dress because it serves a significant purpose. It will help him endure his brutally extensive interviewing schedule. With mathematical brilliancy, he calculates the odds and determines that the likelihood he will happen to be wearing a dress — on the exact interview occasion he might be offered a job — is virtually negligible. In the process, Stanley has learned the valuable lesson his father had sought to teach him, that being a decent human being has nothing to do with clothes and everything to do with the integrity of the individual wearing them.

Stanley has also learned the importance of patience and being persistent. His 99th interview is with Waco Glass and Tile in Pittsburgh. The number is significant in more ways than one. Needless to say, 99 interviews are a lot for a person, with a Ph.D. in mathematics, to have to endure for the prospect of a job in a field such as marketing analysis which was rapidly broadening in the 1940s, with not enough qualified applicants. But the number "99" is also significant because upside down it would be "66," a sign of the Devil. In Linden Hills, Nedeed lives at 999 Tupelo Drive; he is the Devil incarnate, living at the bottom of a soul-troubled community with his symbolically evil address. In the case of Waco Glass and Tile, the evil is of a different nature, but it is an evil just as pervasive as anything that Nedeed represents.

By the time Stanley arrives in Pittsburgh, it is fall and cool enough so that he does not have to wear a dress. Except for his blackness, he can now look the part of a viable job candidate. He initially is interviewed by the "head of domestic marketing" who spends an inordinate amount of time and energy explaining how he is not a racist even as he confirms our suspicions that he actually is. He first points out that he had a black mammy, and then he refers to her children as the "cutest things you'd ever want to see," as if they could just as easily have been chimpanzees instead of human beings. And just as he fails to acknowledge the humanity of his mammy's children, he likewise fails to accept the humanity of the black applicant.

While escorting Stanley to the cafeteria for lunch, that interviewer feels obligated to stop, as Stanley puts it, "at practically every table to introduce my degrees." The head of domestic marketing does not stop at every table to introduce Stanley. He stops to introduce Stanley's academic credentials as if it is the degrees themselves that merit the respect, and not Stanley the person at all.

Then the head of domestic marketing insists that Stanley meet "another good man" who works at the company. This next interviewer holds the position of "second in command at layout and design." We know nothing of his name other than that. And we know that this "good man" is black, the only one thus far who works at the company. The author Earl H. McClenney, in *How to Survive When You're the Only Black in the Office*, offers the following salient advice for blacks who find themselves in a situation such as the one in which Naylor's nameless black executive is placed:

> Black executives are asked to interview blacks for positions even when the position is not in his or her section. White folks seem to think that they are doing something by asking you to interview another black. I remember when I graduated from college I went to work looking for a job with banks and insurance companies in Boston, Mass. Every time I went for an interview, I ended up at some time being interviewed by a black guy. Maybe he was the house nigger. You have to make sure that you don't end up being the house nigger.... Unless you are in a personnel position or a part of a clearly structured interview process, don't get sucked into the token interview and house nigger role.[43]

McClenney, the son of a black college president, bases his conclusions on numerous personal experiences, particularly in the area of public administration. But his depiction of the "house nigger" is nothing new. Malcolm X also was inclined to render the distinction between the "house Negro" and the "field Negro." Specifying that distinction as a carryover from slavery, the Black Muslim leader further explained how the former type of Negro was expected, by the white power structure, to keep the latter type "in check." For his trouble, the house Negro received better housing, better food, and what was in essence a better life.

Identifying himself as one of a multitude of modern field Negroes, Malcolm described the house Negro as one who

> if the master's house caught on fire, the house Negro would fight harder to put the blaze out than the master would. If the master got sick, the house Negro would say, "What's the matter, boss, *we* sick?" *We* sick! He identified himself with his master, more than his master

identified with himself. And if you came to the house Negro and said, "Let's run away, let's escape, let's separate," the house Negro would look at you and say, "Man, you crazy. What you mean, separate? Where is there a better house than this? Where can I wear better clothes than this? Where can I eat better food than this?" That was that house Negro. In those days he was called a "house nigger." And that's what we call them today, because we've still got some house niggers running around here.[44]

McClenney offers the prospect that even if you are the only black person at a company, you do not have to be the "house nigger." But what McClenney does not answer is the obvious question of how does one survive in the corporate work place if he constantly declines the delegated role. If, for example, one continuously refuses to be a token on interview committees, will he thus be perceived as not a "team player," not a valuable enough part of the effort to achieve the corporate goals? Never mind that his role on "the team" is quite different and indeed much more self-deprecating than what the other team players have been called on to do.

The other "good man" in Naylor's novel, the only black thus far who works at the company, is not even thought of by company officials as a free-thinking individual. He is there to fill the role of house nigger, and he thus fulfills the only expectation that the company has for him. As soon as he meets Stanley, he insists, "You're going to love it here," while the head of domestic marketing beams in approval. When the head of domestic marketing asks the second in command, "We treat you right here, don't we?," the black man answers that he is treated "very well." That scenario serves as the modern-day version of a scene from our past where the disgruntled southerner defends his lifestyle with the frantic retort, "All our nigras are happy."

At lunch, Stanley wants to order a steak, but the head of domestic marketing insists that the three of them order lobster thermidor, and we thereby witness another test that is in actuality a continuation of the interview process. Stanley's written proposal is extraordinary and his credentials are impeccable, so the interviewer is compelled to consider this applicant. Yet, in spite of all his talk of Stanley as a "credit to [his] race" and blacks as the "damn finest people in the world," he still does not view him in egalitarian terms as he seeks out just the right reason to deny him employment.

As for the second in command, we learn, interestingly enough, that he is the second in command at layout and design even though he is the *only* person at layout and design. He will never be allowed to be in charge in a department where there is not even another person to offer competition. He is the perennial assistant. He knows when to display a "mild and interested expression"; he knows when to smile. (He wears the mask at least as well as Ellison's Bledsoe.) And when the head of domestic marketing asks him how things are at layout and design, that second in command delivers a hearty "things couldn't be better" response.

In the July 9, 1980 issue of the *Wall Street Journal*, there was an article entitled "Black Executives Say Prejudice Still Impedes Their Path to the Top," where black vice president of First National Bank of Chicago, Clark Burrus, issued the following assessment:

> Back in the old days, people used to joke about "the spook by the door"— the one black employee that many companies hired and put in a highly visible position to show they weren't prejudiced. If things have changed since then, I sure haven't seen it.[45]

Seven years later, McClenney would devote an entire chapter — "HNICs"— to that type of black employee. An age-old term rather common in the black community, HNIC is the abbreviation for "Head Nigger in Charge," and McClenney warns other blacks to stay out of this person's way because under no circumstances can he be trusted.

Then eight years after McClenney's pronouncements, Laurence Otis Graham, in his shocking book *Member of the Club*, included a chapter of his own on the "Head Nigger in Charge" phenomenon. Graham, a 1983 Princeton University and 1988 Harvard Law School graduate, describes:

> The HNIC ... is sometimes elevated to his high status by white bosses who ... recognize a need to appease the media, black consumers, or activists; or who cynically conclude that a token black senior staff person might simultaneously attract government contracts and head off employment discrimination suits by individuals or government agencies.... Today, HNICs are found stuck in various staff positions where they operate with inflated titles that may be as lofty as senior vice president, yet have no staff beyond a secretary, no budget, and no decision-making power within the organization.[46]

That description fits Naylor's second in command to a tee. He has no staff, no budget, no power, and his title is purely inflated. The second in command works in layout and design, but over the past couple of decades in America, we have more characteristically seen such individuals in personnel and public relations departments and affirmative action offices where they, more often than not, have been hired not so much to improve work conditions for black employees, but to protect key executives from outside forces who would force the improvements to occur.

However loyal they may be, blacks who are like Naylor's second in command will never be accepted by those at the top of the corporate hierarchy. The aforementioned *Wall Street Journal* article further asserts "that white corporate executives, comfortable dealing with other whites … haven't tried aggressively to bring blacks into their own elite circle."[47] Actually, that is an understatement. The country club set, where important contacts are met and the big deals are made, has traditionally been off-limits for even the most talented credentialed blacks. Graham, with his two Ivy League degrees, 10 authored books, and $105,000 corporate lawyer salary, was still only able to gain entrance into the country club by posing as a $7-an-hour busboy. And that was not totally surprising since it was fairly common knowledge that black millionaire publisher Earl Graves had years before been rejected from a similar club in spite of his degrees from prestigious institutions and his dizzying business accomplishments.

Graham also devotes a chapter to the matter of dining at New York's top restaurants. These places, where fine cuisine is served, have a dislike for black patrons. As with other things, when it comes to the simple and necessary act of eating, blacks are kept at a distance. And on those occasions when we are invited to share a meal, we are again scrutinized and evaluated for possible defects. The second in command understands the delicacy of this position. Stanley, on the other hand, merely wants to be himself. He drinks wine and martinis and relishes his lobster, cracking its shells with a reckless abandon until the bib he is wearing is a mess. The head of domestic marketing eggs him on in the enjoyment of liquor and lobster. Stanley gets to the point where he first loosens his tie and then takes off his shirt whereupon the second in command finally asks, "What in the high holy *hell* are you doing?"[48] Remember, Stanley is the one who so wanted to be comfortable that he wore dresses to some of his other interviews. Now he is "letting himself go" again.

Within the pages of Bebe Campbell's *New York Times Magazine* article, there is the photograph of an Atlanta corporate manager, Joyce Hicks, standing forlornly in an empty hallway. The picture itself is full of implications. But the caption offers an even more revealing commentary in quoting Hicks as saying, "I've never completely relaxed in the white world."[49]

Why, one might ask, does that continue to be the case in so many black managerial situations? We could look back to Ellison's Dr. Bledsoe who queried the narrator, "Did you forget how to lie?" Lying (or wearing the mask) is, as we have already noted, a long-standing technique of African American survival. It goes back to slavery. The question we are faced with now involves whether or not circumstances have substantially changed in American society to the point where blacks can remove their masks, expose themselves, and not have to worry about callous exploitation as a consequence.

McClenney goes so far as to say that blacks should even stay away from company parties unless it is absolutely necessary for "political reasons related to your job." That seasoned expert further declares:

> If you must go, never drink liquor with your boss or fellow workers. You can pretend. Get yourself a glass of ginger ale or coke.... If you don't drink, you can keep your cool and your head about you. Your mind will be alert to all the things going on.... Be very careful and extremely conservative in what you do and say.[50]

Perhaps Stanley could have benefited from "how-to" advice along the lines of what McClenney provides in his manual. Naylor's interviewee drinks with his prospective boss, loses his composure, and when the second in command asks him, What is he doing?, Stanley replies that he is "getting comfortable," to which the second in command responds, "Are you frigging crazy?"

It is not that Stanley is naive, but he has merely reached the point in his life where he wants to be himself in every situation, corporate setting or not. He is not like Ellison's invisible man who, upon his arrival in New York, rejected the wholesome southern meal of pork chops, grits, and biscuits. As hungry as Ellison's character probably was, he settled instead for orange juice, toast, and coffee. That choice by the narrator reminds us somewhat of the delicately refined eating habits of the upwardly mobile residents of Linden Hills. But unlike Maxwell Smyth, Roxanne Tilson, and other Linden Hill residents, Ellison's narrator will eventually recant his self-denying culinary practices. Having been formerly ashamed of black southern cultural foods, he can now walk down the street, eating a hot candied yam out in the open for all to see as he asserts his identity declaring, "I yam what I am!"

And this is the point where Stanley is in his personal development. As he is eating his lobster thermidor, one imagines he does it with all the enjoyment of blacks gathering around a table to indulge in a meal of pig feet or crabs or fried chicken so greasy that a person has to lick his fingers afterward to finish enjoying the meal. There are no inhibitions, just fully partaking of life. After all, the rest of his name is Beckwourth Booker T. Washington Carver. He has an identity to uphold that is steeped in African American culture. And he can no more deny his birthright than the invisible man who declares the yam as his "birthmark" and contemplates:

> What and how much had I lost by trying to do only what was expected of me instead of what I myself had wished to do? . . . It involved a problem of choice.... I had accepted the accepted attitudes.[51]

Stanley and the invisible man conduct this reassessment, but how about Naylor's second in command? He seems to be not that much concerned about the emotional cost he is paying to keep his corporate position. On the other hand, perhaps he has questioned himself along the lines of what Johnson's ex-coloured man asks as he ponders whether or not "I have sold my birthright for a mess of pottage."[52] If indeed the second in command has posited such a question to himself, whatever he concluded, he is still able to carry on pandering to the white bosses in terms of what they expect of him as a black man.

There is a great deal of ambiguity in Stanley's father's assertion that "change is hope," for as Stanley acknowledges, "We are on the brink of unimaginable possibilities."[53] There in the 1940s, the atom is about to be split and the world is at the advent of nuclear energy. And still we are a world in which people, both in body and spirit, are sold to the highest bidder. This is what the second in command represents. The tragedy becomes clearer as we hear Stanley tell his father that "change" is beginning to worry him because "today I had lunch with the future." For the 99th time, he lost the prospect of a job. But that was the 1940s when discrimination against blacks was almost a national pastime.

What of the present? Well, it is worth noting that several Chicago-based researchers, in their 1991 essay entitled "We'd Love to Hire Them, But ...," found that white companies in general perceive blacks as being "unskilled, uneducated, illiterate, dishonest, lacking initiative, unmotivated ... unstable, lacked a work ethic, and had no family life or role models."[54] The stereotypes enumerated in that perception seem so familiar because combined they comprise some of the same rationales that were used to perpetuate slavery. And now well over a century after the abolition of the "peculiar institution," it might very well be the case that the perception of blacks has not changed.

At lunch, Stanley is unable to take his eyes off of the second in command's paper bib that, throughout the lobster meal, had remained spotless. Stanley and the head of domestic marketing had been given a bib also, but theirs became thoroughly splattered in the process of eating. Unlike his fellow diners, the second in command "took very small bites" of his lobster. He is familiar with "the routine" and knows that much more important than him enjoying his meal is the importance of denying himself and being viewed by his superiors as just the right black to be used as a foil in case another black person accuses the company of discrimination. He is "proof" that Waco Glass and Tile does not discriminate. And so it goes from one generation to another and on into infinity.

"Torn Asunder": Brent Wade's Portrayal of Human Disintegration

W.E.B. Du Bois's oft-quoted, prophetic announcement in *The Souls of Black Folk* that

> the Negro is a sort of seventh son, born with a veil, and gifted with second-sight in this American world, — a world which yields him no true self-consciousness, but only lets him see himself through the revelation of the other world. It is a peculiar sensation, this double-consciousness, this sense of always looking at one's self through the eyes of others, of measuring one's soul by the tape of a world that looks on in amused contempt and pity. One ever feels his two-ness, — an American, a Negro; two souls, two thoughts, two unreconciled strivings; two warring ideals in one dark body, whose dogged strength alone keeps it from being torn asunder[1]

is necessary for us to reconsider here as we seek to comprehend the essence of African American identity. The notion of double-consciousness is an especially appropriate perspective from which to evaluate the psychological state of African Americans. Or put another way, in the process of cultural prioritization, are we black first or are we primarily American? Still, many will argue that the question itself is inappropriate, for no human being should be placed in the position of having to make such a choice.

But what Du Bois was arguing in 1903, is that the choice has already been made. Whites in America have so dominated the culture and controlled the wealth, that to be considered a part of the American mainstream, there must be substantial adherence, on the part of the individual, to a generally perceived societal norm. We will recall John T. Molloy's stipulation that the "typical upper-middle-class American looks white." Well, although blacks have made significant inroads into the American middle class, we still are not proportionately represented, and our inroads into the upper middle class are even more drastically disproportionate. And regardless of any black achievement, the wealthiest segment of the general population is nearly always symbolized by a well-dressed, silver-haired, middle-aged white man. That is the image and that is the reality. The relatively few blacks who have risen to the highest socioeconomic plateaus have usually done so by convincing the public (in a manner not very much unlike Johnson's ex-coloured man) that they are as "white" as anybody else, or that they are as willing as the white majority to downplay the major black issues.

Blacks are just as interested in being successful as anyone else, but as we analyze what the price is that must be paid for that success, we can better understand the depths of meaning behind Du Bois's phraseology: "two warring ideals"; "measuring one's soul by the tape of a world that looks on in amused contempt." Contemplating such an existence is painful enough. But to feel it, to actually be restricted to that aforementioned life of duality with "no true self-consciousness" is a circumstance that is almost too bizarre to convey with mere words.

Du Bois fathomed that there is, on the part of African Americans, a "dogged strength" that keeps us "from being torn asunder." But he was being much too optimistic. If the truth be told, it would have to be said that the various individuals of the black race respond differently to the social cataclysm. Many do endure with their psyches intact. Others react with uncontrollable rage. And then there are those who can somehow find the means to conceal their emotions as they quietly go insane.

In *Bailey's Cafe*, the second in command had a spotless bib even after eating his lobster dinner. While domestic marketing rambles on about how wonderful a place Waco Glass and Tile is for blacks, the second in command begins shredding his paper bib into "tiny tiny tiny tiny pieces. When the bib was intact, Stanley could not take his eyes off of it; it was a wonder to behold while others' bibs were being thoroughly splattered. But as the second in command tears up his bib, Stanley "forced [himself] to look everywhere but there; it was becoming something indecent to watch."[2] Of course there is more going on here than just the rending into pieces of a spotless bib. We are witnesses also to a tragedy, for it is while that second in command is agreeing with anything domestic marketing says, that he tears at the bib, an act of displacement on the part of the former that is symbolic of the rending of his very own soul.

As I have already noted, it is this process of displacement that enables the second in command to survive emotionally in spite of the kowtowing role that he plays. Unfortunately, William Covington, in Brent Wade's novel *Company Man*, is not so adept at survival. In fact, as the novel opens, we find him wasting away in a psychiatric ward, writing in his journal, in part as a means of making reparations for the time when he rejected Paul Walker. Walker, high school classmate and fellow track team member, is also Covington's cousin. Yet, Covington chose to reject this relative once it became clear he was homosexual. Covington denounced Walker without so much as a second thought, but now, isolated in a mental ward with time for contemplation, he writes in his journal, seeking to solve the riddle of his cousin's identity:

> Were you a homosexual even then or was it something that developed later during the summer before your first year of college? I've never had the guts to ask you until now or, for that matter, ask you just what it is to be that way. I've heard different things. Is it a way of thinking, or something else?[3]

Like Ellison's naive narrator, Covington has never before had to face the issue of homosexuality in terms of its psychological and biological make-up. The last question in that quote is another way of asking what has become a rather typical query: Are homosexuals born the way they are, or is it a choice they made? Whenever I raise that question as an issue in my classes, my homosexual students immediately snap back at me: "If there was a choice, considering the way that homosexuals are ostracized, why would anyone *choose* to be homosexual?" That answer is always sufficient for me, but the question still lingers in this homophobic culture, and it is only at the point of Covington's institutionalization that he ponders the prospect that society's rejection of his cousin's homosexuality is similar to society's rejection of African Americans.

This strategy of using homosexuality as a gauge for alienation was also employed by J.D. Salinger in *The Catcher in the Rye*. In that novel, Mr. Antolini is one of only a few adults who are sensitive enough and responsive to Holden Caulfield's dilemma of self-identification. But then later, when he is sleeping on Antolini's couch, he:

> woke up all of a sudden.... I felt something on my head, some guy's hand.... What it was, it was Mr. Antolini's hand. What he was

doing, he was sitting on the floor right next to the couch, in the
dark and all, and he was sort of petting me or patting me on the
goddam head.[4]

Salinger makes it absolutely ambiguous as to whether or not Antolini
is fondling Caulfield or whether he is merely attempting to comfort the
young man through a turbulent period. But the point is that Caulfield
does not weigh the possible explanations for Antolini's action. Instead,
he labels Antolini a pervert and refuses to associate any further with
him.

As is the case with Covington and Walker and the invisible man
and young Emerson, it is unfortunate that Caulfield does not take
advantage of the opportunity to fully analyze the circumstances of those
who are forced to live with a homosexual stigma. Each of our three
protagonists might have learned a great deal about their own disad-
vantageous social positions had they been more open-minded in their
considerations of others who are similarly situated. The very fact that
they are willing to disregard what Ellison referred to as "the possibilities," makes them essentially hypocritical, capable of the same sort of
phoniness that Caulfield decried throughout the pages of Salinger's
novel.

But phoniness is evident in each of our lives, a natural by-prod-
uct of the fear we have that we might suddenly, without warning, be
deprived of whatever prosperity and self-assurance we may have been
able to attain in our lives. The incontrovertible fact though is that even
supposed security is limited. As Bob Slocum's boss tells him in *Something Happened*:

> You're not a free citizen as long as you're working for me. ... You
> wouldn't be able to get a better job without my help, and you
> wouldn't be able to take it if you did. You'd have to give up your
> pension and profit sharing.... You're dependent on me.... You have
> to grovel every time I want you to.[5]

Such a state of affairs makes us urgently aware of how important it is
to become indispensable in each of our particular employment situations. For Lucius Brockway, in *Invisible Man*, a crucial point in his
career comes when he has the opportunity to help the company
president devise a corporate slogan. And the slogan that came to characterize not only Liberty Paints but also (through Ellison's use of

symbolism) America as a whole was "If It's Optic White, It's the Right White," a thinly veiled variation of the more widely applied expression, "If you're white, you're right."

Brockway of course sells his soul. But he is only human. He wants to eat; he wants to thrive. And in so doing he personifies the metaphor of soul-selling that has been passed down through the ages, whether it be Marlowe's Doctor Faustus, Goethe's Faust, Johnson's ex-coloured man, or Naylor's Luther Nedeed.

And now comes William Covington, falling in line with the same tradition. He provides the slogan for Varitech Corporation, a company composed mainly of engineers who produce "specialized machinery" for the electronics industry. The slogan that he suggests is "Building the Future's Foundation, Today," and John Haviland, only a general manager at the time, supports it through the various evaluative levels until it is finally adopted.

Covington gets credit for the motto, but we can be sure that Haviland gets his share of credit too for discovering the man who created the saying. And while not as obviously detrimental to blacks as Brockway's credo, Covington's slogan is just as racially flawed. Varitech Corporation has an unwritten policy of training whites first, on new specialized equipment; they get promoted first, and when jobs are lost to Mexico, it is those white employees who are least likely to be laid off as a consequence. If this is how the foundation for the future is being built — "today," as the corporate slogan goes — then it is certainly not a foundation of which blacks at the company can be proud. The slogan for them is a farce.

Yet, Covington, himself a black man, is the one who created the slogan. One is reminded of the scene in *Invisible Man* at Liberty Paints where it takes 10 drops of black liquid added to a substance to make it "glossy white." Such a phenomenon defies reason. How can black added to a "milky brown" substance make it white? But here Ellison is being symbolic again. The 10 drops of black liquid represent the approximate percentage of the American population that blacks comprise. We need only recall what Ellison had said about the "presence of black Americans" being used "as a marker, a symbol of limits," in order to understand how much white superiority depends on black confirmation.

Perhaps Covington does not understand all that he is getting himself into as he subjects himself to the process of being used to support the existing white corporate structure. He cannot possibly understand everything as he is wading through the corporate mire. However, in retrospect, he does now comprehend the full extent of the subtle deal that he made. Writing to Walker in his journal, he admits, "That slogan was really the beginning of my career at Varitech because through that one act I gained John Haviland's patronage."[6] Then Covington, still writing in his journal, goes on to explain:

> You must understand the nature of patronage.... what the patron requires most from the recipient is loyalty. The more loyalty displayed, the more opportunity the patron will bestow, since this loyalty, however mercenary, is the only real external security the patron can have against the atavism of corporate life.... the more power the patron grants, the greater the loyalty demanded.[7]

Covington had entered into the game of one favor for another, accumulating "chips," you-scratch-my-back-I'll-scratch-yours ass-kissing as the essential mode to insure survival in the corporation. It is a game that most people must play in some form or another if they hope to advance up the organizational hierarchy. But blacks are in an even more peculiar position. As Covington expresses in his journal, Haviland "knew that my loyalty was perhaps more assured than most, since his offer was the only one I was likely to receive."[8] Having started out at Varitech as a speechwriter, he will begin the ascendancy that is his reward for contributing the company slogan. Yet, due to the nature of past discrimination, there are not many places he can serve. The path of advancement is narrow for Covington and every other black at the company. And thus we see how the patronage-loyalty dynamic is even more important for blacks than for whites who have historically been provided with a wider variety of support mechanisms.

In interviewing black corporate managers for a 1982 *Ebony* article, Bebe Moore Campbell received the following response from one black manager who worked for a large energy company in Richmond, Virginia:

> If I asked a question, my supervisor would give me a basic answer. If my White counterpart asked a question, they'd give him the whole picture.[9]

That manager complained about not being included in the "network," an informal system of contacts within an organization whereby certain individuals are favored over others and consequently given the greater opportunities. In some places it is called "office politics." Covington refers to it as the "old boy system." But by whatever name, it must be seen as no different than say the ordinary grade school teacher who favors one child over another because he cleans the erasers, tattles on classmates, or hails from a prominent family. The game is the same even if at Varitech the players are older and the stakes are so much higher.

In any situation of human interaction, something similar takes place. During times of legal segregation, for example, blacks had their own "pecking order" system where certain individuals were groomed, based on skin color, for specific privileged positions within the black community. Kathy Russell, Midge Wilson, and Ronald Hall — in their eye-opening psycho-sociological study *The Color Complex* — reveal a centuries-long process whereby black churches, schools, and other organizations systematically excluded certain members of their race to the point where, as the researchers tell us, "churches painted their doors a light shade of brown, and anyone whose skin was darker than the door was politely invited to seek religious services elsewhere."[10] Those authors go on to confirm the tragic reality that, even now, due to the support mechanisms that have been long ensconced in the American culture, light-skinned blacks fare better than their darker skinned counterparts in the effort to gain status across a wide range of fields including business, politics, and higher education.

One might say then that at least the light-skinned blacks have no reason to complain. Within the context of their community — that is, the black community — they are in a favored position. But what people seem to forget so easily these days is that a large part of the modern Civil Rights Movement was designed to break down the walls that had previously separated the races so rigidly. Freedom is not relative. You cannot be free in one isolated, confined corner of the world. You can only be free on an at-large basis. This requirement is inherent in freedom's definition. So to be privileged — on only one side of town — means, for all intent and purposes, nothing if society as a whole accords you the status of a leper.

To a large extent, the Civil Rights Movement was about making inroads into the unchartered territory of a foreboding white world. Skin tone, though a factor, would not be so important as whether or not you were a "good nigger" or a "bad nigger." These were the two basic types that white people used to distinguish and categorize the largely unknown black racial entity. Before the 1960s, most whites did not concern themselves with the complexities of black existence. And they certainly would not have known that, within the context of the black community, we discriminated against our own kind based on skin color. We had become, in terms of psychological make-up, more like them than anyone might ever have imagined.

And yet we were indeed a community, forced to work together and organize so that we might advance even though the pace was very slow and measurable only in the smallest of increments. So when Covington gets his job as a speechwriter at Varitech, he is fulfilling the collective dream of those who for generations had been denied opportunity. Yet, he is still an outsider. He creates the company slogan, and Haviland is prepared to reward him for this, but not without a price. That white executive was himself on the "fast track," destined to be president of the company one day. Covington might prove himself to be an invaluable asset as Haviland climbs to the utmost corporate rung. But the question remains: Can Haviland count on Covington's unwavering loyalty?

The manager (that Campbell interviewed) at the energy company in Virginia was disturbed about not being made privy to the same information that was afforded white managers in the organization. And therein lies the great difficulty. If the system was originally set up to exclude African Americans, how will it be when the occasion arrives that one or two blacks are brought in? John Molloy, the dress-for-success expert, is correct in assessing that blacks, in order to be accepted, will have to adhere to the corporate dress code even more stringently than what would be expected from others. But conformity to a dress standard is not quite enough. In further explaining the corporate patronage system to his cousin Walker, Covington writes:

> To understand this is to understand why the top jobs at Varitech (and probably a lot of American companies) seem historically peopled by men strikingly similar to one another. Executives are most likely to trust what they're familiar with.[11]

Having only recently arrived on the corporate scene, in the managerial sense, how do blacks go about gaining access to the all-important network? How do we get the promotions, the raises, the vital pieces of information that are the evidence of success in this "world" where savvy is more important than any college-taught skill?

Citing studies conducted by the Olsten Corporation, the Human Resource Planning Society, and the Center for Creative Leadership, *Jet* magazine, in 1993, issued the report that "white managers," in general, "close the door on people they are not comfortable with and they choose successors who will maintain those hiring practices."[12] Quoting directly from one of those studies, *Jet* further informed that a "surprisingly small number" of companies are actively engaged in programs of diversification because white managers are more comfortable "with their own kind." That is the tragic reality regardless of what the various companies say about their efforts at being all-inclusive. Covington knows it. Blacks who have been turned away know it. And indeed, Haviland and other white managers who wield the power in large corporations know that blacks in managerial positions are there, for the most part, to provide the window dressing.

On the issue of loyalty, Covington phrases the matter quite well in declaring that Haviland could be relatively assured of his loyalty since opportunities for blacks to participate in the patronage system are relatively scarce compared to what white initiates are offered. In promoting Covington from speechwriter to executive assistant, Haviland is making an astute tactical move. He can appear to be breaking new ground in terms of race relations while providing himself with a safety net when the masses of blacks who are at the lower levels complain about discriminatory practices.

But before placing Covington on the fast track, Haviland will have to test him. Covington got his foot in the door by devising the corporate slogan. But the depths of his loyalty to Varitech, and Haviland in particular, have yet to be ascertained. That is when Haviland decides to invite Covington and his wife, Paula, to the marketing department's Christmas party where the former will blurt out, with regard to the latter's wife, "She's a gorgeous woman. Are both her parents black?"[13] What, one might ask, does a man's wife have to do with his company-related performance? Covington, in his journal, explains the phenomenon quite well:

> Having a beautiful wife is an asset in the corporate world. For the rising young executives, it's quietly looked upon as one of the rewards of good cocksmanship. There's an attendant prestige for the man with a beautiful wife. Her beauty gets extrapolated somehow into a presumption of his good salesmanship, good marketing skills, or some larger savvy ... the wife gets reduced to an accoutrement.[14]

This is a novel about the late 1980s, and we can observe how, even for this college-educated woman, her intelligence is not deemed as important as her looks. We are reminded of Zora Neale Hurston's *Their Eyes Were Watching God* when Janie Crawford is asked to make a speech and her husband Joe Starks interrupts the proceedings to declare, "Mah wife don't know nothin' 'bout no speech-makin'. Ah never married her for nothin' lak dat."[15] Starks himself is a man who is determined to be a "big voice." His plan is to "buy in big" at the place, soon to be Eatonville, where "colored folks was buildin' theirselves." He had been saving money for years, anticipating just the right moment.

But as crucial as it was for him to have a sound financial base, it was just as important for him to have an attractive wife. That was his purpose in marrying Janie. With her light skin and straight hair, she proves just the ornament he needs to be a leader in the developing town. True, he has a certain savvy in terms of being able to determine how best to take advantage of the townfolks' naivete, but with Janie at his side, he is perceived as having what Covington refers to as "some larger savvy," having harnessed a woman with beauty. Men like Amos Hicks believe they are just as capable as Starks in terms of doing all that he was able to accomplish. "Mah britches is just as long as his," Hicks asserts. But it is the lack of a woman, who looks like Janie, that is his major drawback. "But dat wife uh hisn!" he regretfully acknowledges, "Ah'm uh son of uh Combunction if Ah don't go tuh Georgy and git me one just like her."[16] The implication is that, in Georgia, the women will be lighter, prettier, and thereby better assets for men to possess on their way up the social ladder.

Covington accepts this feature of corporate life and, in doing so, confirms the socially perceived notion of women as inferior beings. But beyond even that, Paula has been insulted as a black woman. Because she is light-skinned with green eyes, Haviland asks the extremely personal question, "Are both her parents black?" Covington, in retrospect, acknowledges that Haviland would never have even asked another black person such a question; but Haviland asks *him*. "It was," as Covington notes, "a way of confirming things." Haviland can say anything, however insulting, to Covington and he will accept it, wear a "pleasant puppet smile" and carry on as if nothing out of the ordinary has happened. Since white managers are more comfortable rewarding "their own kind," the burden shifts to Covington to prove that he is all right, one of *them*, willing to deny his essential being for corporate success.

As Covington assesses it, blacks of previous generations never had to undergo that particular type of self-degradation. He, for example, does not believe his own father-in-law could "appreciate how difficult it is to sustain a sense of dignity in the corporate world — and stay employed."[17] Regardless of race, lower-level employees have to kowtow to their superiors in various direct and indirect ways. The position of blacks in the corporate world is even more tenuous because of the perception that we only got the position as a gratuity and we in return should be grateful for the privilege of being employed. We are not owed the same respect as a white person in a similar employment situation. Covington's father, on the other hand, is one of those light-skinned medical doctors whose position as a professional was limited to the black community that understood him and was inclined to "look in awe upon" him as a "racial spokesman." Segregated as he was from the white world, he did not have to worry about whether he was lackeying hard enough to hold on to his job.

When Haviland asked Covington whether or not Paula's parents were black, Covington could have responded in one of several ways. He might have said simply, "Yes, her parents were indeed black," and left the matter at that. Such a reply would have been a capitulation of sorts, but not the most self-degrading of possible responses. Had he been braver he might have rejected the appropriateness of Haviland's question and demanded to know "why her parentage mattered at all." If he had been even more courageous he would have gone on ahead and explained his wife's light colored skin and "recessive" green eyes and

added a little discourse on the all-too-widespread concubine status that many black slave women had held, that Thomas Jefferson himself was guilty of this, and that this practice accounts for the various skin and eye shadings of modern black Americans. I could have also pointed out that his apparent ignorance of this fact was evidence of the short shrift the black experience is given in the education and minds of Americans.[18]

Of course, had Covington given that response he would have been indirectly indicting Haviland for the concubinage phenomenon that was practiced if not by his own ancestors then certainly by others of his race in previous generations. By including Thomas Jefferson among the men who were culpable, Covington would have been disparaging one of America's most heralded leaders — Founding Father, creator of the *Declaration of Independence,* and irreproachable in the minds of many white Americans. Had Covington lambasted Haviland, publicly declaring him ignorant of the black experience, it would probably have cost him the patronage he is so desperately seeking.

But Covington gives none of those responses. Instead, he eagerly answers his superior by first informing him that both of her parents are black and then he adds, "She's just very light complexioned. It's pretty common."[19] No accusations. No innuendoes. Just a simple pat answer to a question that in itself was full of complexly racist overtones. By answering as he does though, Covington makes Haviland comfortable, gets promoted to executive assistant, and soon thereafter becomes director of marketing communications, all because he understood the "long-term benefit of guarding [his] tongue."

As prestigious as that title sounds, one is inclined to question what will be the nature of his new duties. He himself acknowledges that "marketing communications was looked upon largely as a helpful but not entirely necessary part of the business."[20] In other words, he is expendable. Reflecting back now, from his room on the psychiatric ward, he contemplates the rationale whereby he allowed himself to be reconciled with his new position:

> While my role at the boardroom meetings and long-term market-planning sessions may have been diaphanous (if not invisible), all in all it was a pleasant, comfortable rut. There was a certain coital snugness about it. I had a great salary, the patronage of the company president, a beautiful wife, a handsome old house, and a cardinal red XJ6.[21]

Material possessions had taken precedence over any other kind of need Covington might have had for a fulfilling employment experience. The "beautiful wife," as has been duly noted, was just another one of those possessions. He is director of marketing communications but it is a "diaphanous" position, a role that is virtually meaningless within the corporate structure since while he is director of marketing he nonetheless makes no marketing decisions. He is Varitech's version of Naylor's second in command of layout and design who is allocated neither budget, nor staff, nor actual power.

Though invisible as far as Varitech's decision-making processes are concerned, just as had been the case with the second in command, Covington will be trotted out whenever the company needs someone to draw attention away from its traditionally racist hiring practices. In a unit of 2,800 employees, there are only four black managers. Sooner or later, black employees will complain. But with Covington available to rebut the complaint, the company can go on with business as usual. White executives need only refer to him as the evidence that progress is being made in terms of minority hiring. That is the purpose that Covington serves, and as Haviland rises through the corporate ranks, he also paves the way for his flunky.

Writing about black lawyers who work for white corporations, Harvard Law School professor David Wilkins points to the "danger that black lawyers who choose to work in this area will fail to contribute to the struggle to end the unjustified inequalities between blacks and whites, and may indirectly or directly help perpetuate them."[22] One of the paradoxes that Wilkins has in mind is the situation where a black lawyer is assigned to defend his company against the charge of racial discrimination. Should the lawyer decline? Should he resign from his law firm completely? In such a situation, what is his obligation to the black community? I find it rather intriguing that Wilkins gives no precise answer in terms of what that lawyer should do.

Black employees at Varitech are on the verge of a strike that will seriously interfere with company operations. And Haviland asks Covington to spy. "I need you on the inside," is how the CEO puts it. Whether or not he recognizes that such act on the part of Covington will be tantamount to betrayal, he is capable of characterizing the spying as a responsibility that Covington owes to the company. If Covington accedes to his boss's wishes, he will be, as Wilkins put it, directly helping to perpetuate unjustified inequality. Haviland is extremely insensitive, for he can, without inhibition, urge Covington, "If there's something else at issue here tell me."[23] That CEO seems not to know or not to care that as he makes this demand he burdens his mentee with an emotionally destructive dilemma.

We should consider here how Haviland symbolizes, to some extent, all of white America which has eagerly courted those African Americans who were willing to portray the nation as having made steady progress toward resolving the race question. As important, for example, as the 1963 March on Washington was, even that event must be reevaluated in light of Malcolm X's accusation that politically powerful whites "controlled it so tight, they told those Negroes what time to hit town, how to come, where to stop, what signs to carry, what song to sing, what speech they could make, and what speech they couldn't make; and then told them to get out of town by sundown."[24] Of course we could say that in providing a setting for the speeches to take place, white leaders were merely accommodating a milestone event in the Civil Rights Movement. But if it was as Malcolm characterized it, that whites decided who the specific speakers would be, then what took place on that August afternoon — between the Lincoln Memorial and the Washington Monument — was not so much the offer of white assistance but the insistence on white control.

Yet it is frightening to contemplate what life would be like had there been no Martin Luther King, Jr. Moreover, the William Covingtons of the world have made their own vital contributions. Even as Wilkins indicates how black corporate lawyers can perpetuate discrimination, those very same lawyers might still provide a positive impact. They inspire other blacks, make inroads into politics, and by the sheer power of their personal achievements, they refute the old stereotype of blacks as intellectually inferior.

But Wilkins is concerned with how corporate blacks might wind up in a dangerously paradoxical position. They can easily fall prey to the HNIC traps which Laurence Otis Graham outlines in categorical fashion to include, for example, the "affirmative action deal closer," the "colorless dreamer," the "expedient African American," and the "two-faced henchman." Every black manager who falls into those categories suffers from acute emotional stress because by fulfilling their white employers' needs, they have "moved away" from themselves.

This is how Covington assesses his emotional dismantlement. At one point having denied any knowledge of the black machinists' strike-related activities, he finally gives in and tells Haviland all that he knows. And at that very instant, we witness the psychological phenomenon of a man being disattached from himself. Covington recalls:

> As I talked a heaviness slowly enveloped me. It was pressing me downward and then it gave, releasing me. I was moving away from myself. I heard myself talking, knew what I was saying, could feel myself thinking, but at the same time I was apart. Unable to affect what was happening but aware of it, observing it almost. Voices and sounds began to take on an elongated quality, ascending away from me.[25]

This climactic point in the novel actually had its beginnings at the Christmas party when Covington had responded so eagerly to Haviland's question about Paula's parentage; the unspoken agreement was sealed. Haviland reaped the benefits of that deal while for Covington, it was "like the first step in a duel wherein I would eventually have to turn and stare myself in the face."[26] Du Bois called it "two warring ideals in one dark body." Covington calls it a duel, a battle between two opposing forces wherein one must of necessity be eliminated by the other though they are both part of one human being.

Having received vital inside information about the black machinists' plans, the CEO then tells Covington he wants him to sabotage the group's efforts at forming a union. As though it was not bad enough that he was forced to be Haviland's spy, Covington is now expected to personally thwart the black machinists' organizing efforts.

Among Graham's types of HNIC's is "the informant" who "serves a valuable but self-destroying function." From the whites' perspective he is extremely valuable. But as he finds himself being forced to betray other blacks, he winds up in the position of undermining his own integrity to such a degree that he looms unrecognizable even to himself. To outward appearances he is the successful corporate officer. Yet internally, within his own psyche, he hates the creature he has become and despises the things he has had to do to ensure his corporate survival.

The point at which Covington is ordered to waylay other blacks in the midst of their organizing strategies is the point at which he loses his sanity. Naylor's Maxwell Smyth had urged Xavier Donnell to maintain his balance up on the "tightrope." Now we find Covington writing in his journal that "at some point you have to wake up from the high-wire act of your cognitive dissonance to the fact that the net beneath you is made of smoke."[27] Covington, who had at one time been able to maintain his balance as a black corporate executive, now finds himself plunging into an abyss, that no-man's land of personal insecurity from which he never had adequate protection.

As he ponders his emotional state, he realizes that his dilemma actually began long ago with his grandmother who demanded that he not act "niggerish." Unlike Laurel Dumont's grandmother who symbolized a proud black heritage, Covington's grandmother represents those blacks who are ashamed of their Afrocentricity. As Covington reveals:

> The year we were told that we would begin junior high in an integrated school, she began to push me to emulate white speech.... what she dreamt for was my metamorphosis into a Generic, a man devoid of any cultural affiliation.[28]

Devoid of color was what Maxwell Smyth had wanted. But to be devoid of either color or "cultural affiliation," in a society that is dominated by whites, means submission to the dominant culture. Covington's grandmother wanted her grandson to undergo the "metamorphosis" because she believed that was blacks' best chance to rise above the limitations of previous generations. In a sense she is like Janie Crawford's Nanny who arranged for her granddaughter to marry Logan Killicks so that she could have financial security. And just as, in the process, Nanny denied Janie the chance to be her own woman, Covington's grandmother denied him the chance to be his own man.

In the final analysis, it is indeed the status of Covington's manhood that is at issue in Wade's novel. As he gave himself to the patronage process and consequently rose rapidly through the corporate ranks, he equated his situation to that of a man engaged in sexual intercourse, describing his position as one of "coital snugness." But he was of course deceiving himself. Engaged as he is in this corporate process, he has relinquished his personal autonomy and caused us to question how his manhood could possibly be left intact.

The actor Ossie Davis, in explaining why he eulogized Malcolm X, said Malcolm "knew that every Negro who did not challenge on the spot every instance of racism, overt or covert, committed against him and his people, who chose instead to swallow his spit and go on smiling, was an Uncle Tom and a traitor, without balls or guts, or any other commonly accepted aspects of manhood!"[29] In the eulogy itself, Davis called Malcolm, "Our manhood.... our black shining Prince." Why the emphasis on manhood? And why was it so important to have had Malcolm as an example of that physical and psychological state? For the answer to those questions, it is essential to look back at the era of slavery when black men were not allowed to be men. They could protect neither their wives nor their children, either of whom might have been beaten, sold, or raped right in the black man's presence without him having any recourse, legal or otherwise, short of a suicidal assault on the master.

Though some did, few black men chose that option. We opted instead for survival. Once slavery ended, not much changed in terms of the deference that blacks were expected to show toward whites. Having to submit to this system was a brutalizing process both for black women and men. But in the mainstream culture, the definition of manhood included that he be in possession of substantial authority. In this respect, the brutalization process was more devastating for black men (even as black women were being raped by white men) because while black women were not denied their womanhood, black men were denied their manhood and left with no identity at all.

One finds the emasculation process continuing even today as often the price for success is to deny your own manhood to remain in the good graces of an immediate superior. Caught in this predicament, Heller's Bob Slocum laments, "I cannot for the very life and dignity of me, feel anything inside my undershorts where my exterior sexual organs are supposed to be."[30] Here we have the evidence that others, besides black men, have been rendered impotent by the prevailing dehumanizing corporate methodologies.

Yet it is vital to consider something else that Ossie Davis said: "White folks do not need anybody to remind them that they are men. We do!"[31] At various stages of American history, blacks were legally classified as three fifths of a person or not even a person at all, but rather as chattel property, of no more significance than plantation livestock. One does not overcome such a stigma by the mere passage of an Emancipation Proclamation or any of the other numerous bills and executive orders that have been handed down over the past century ostensibly to redress the horrid evil that slavery and subsequent racial subjugation imposed.

So the sexual impotency — that Covington soon realizes has been a problem unfolding in his psyche further back than even he can remember — is different from the impotency that Slocum suffers. There is never any question as to whether or not Slocum is a human being, as ineffectual as he may be in the corporate setting. On the other hand, once Covington is deprived of his sexual prowess, there is nothing else to confirm his status as either a man or a human being. He can no longer satisfy his wife. When black men had nothing else in this world, we had the private knowledge — though indeed paradoxically nurtured by racism and its accompanying stereotypes — that in the confines of our bedrooms, we could succeed at this if nothing else. And this was how we achieved manhood, staked out a place within the realm of humanity. This is why Covington refers to his fit within the corporation as a "coital snugness." Successful sexuality, however symbolic, is essential to who he is.

But once he is required to perform the traitorous task, he loses what is left of identity. The psychotherapist declares, "Your problem could be purely psychological or it could be part of a larger physiological disorder."[32] That analyst is capable enough to suspect that the problem might be job related, that Covington is undergoing "unusual stress." And in suggesting that the problem could be part of a "larger physiological disorder," he approaches as precise an evaluation as could ever be possible from someone unfamiliar with Du Bois's version of the split-personality phenomenon.

Covington describes his own mental breakdown as the point "where the lights went out." And there in the darkness, he ponders these crucial questions:

> Hadn't my entire life been a pilgrimage to this place? It's where you end up when you divide yourself, and it's haunted by the ghost of that other, the invisible man I kept interred in the ivory shell. Who was he that we should not have stood together in such a long time?[33]

The "invisible man" to whom Covington refers is the mask that many blacks are still compelled to don as we negotiate our progress in a racially hostile society. We are Brer Rabbits who risk being ourselves only during cloistered moments when we are free from the permeating dangers.

What worried Du Bois so much was that by becoming invisible, we ultimately lose parts of ourselves. We become the act, so to speak, even while we struggle to reconcile the dual consciousness. Covington grapples with the task and we watch on in awe as he apparently becomes three different people, "all one part of a larger body, this brooding fecund unconsumable blackness."[34] He seems to be speaking for blacks in general as he painfully declares we "will never be fully assimilated." Blackness "will always stand abject and separate.... as the depreciated reciprocal of whatever whiteness has come to mean."[35] That resounding proclamation seems not to be all that different from the Ellisonian notion of whiteness being defined by the presence of blackness. But Ellison was a great deal more optimistic in his anticipation of the great American melting pot. On the other hand, neither Du Bois nor Wade give any evidence of an end to the emotional trauma either internally (in one human being) or between the black and white races.

As Covington reaches the climax of his struggle, he becomes William and Billy and Bill. He was born William, and this is the only name that his grandmother called him in her effort to engender prestige in the boy. Much more interesting, however, is the distinction between "Bill" and "Billy," a distinction that has its basis in cultural difference. Blacks call him "Billy"; whites call him "Bill." A comparable phenomenon is evidenced in the way that blacks might refer to a lover as "baby" while whites use the appellation "babe." The former has a drawn out, lingering melodic sound; the latter is much more abrupt. More importantly though, as between "Bill" and "Billy," Covington seems not to have a very good idea which one he is. And if he is both, he does not know which he prefers. He has become lost to himself even as he sought to belong in the world.

By the end of the novel, we find him dragging his three selves into the office of Carl Rice, a black manager who is openly critical of the white power structure and facilitates the efforts of the black machinists. It is here that Covington seems to have some measure of emotional success, for right there in front of Rice, he signs the petition. Not only does he sign it, but he signs it at the top of the page where Haviland and all the other higher-ups at Varitech can clearly see it. The pronoun "we," that Wade had been using to portray Covington's psychological disjointedness, now becomes "I." He is able to have sex with his wife. He appears to have accomplished what Ossie Davis said Malcolm, in his own way, did for so many in that "you always left his presence with the sneaky suspicion that maybe, after all, you *were* a man!"[36]

But Covington's progress is short-lived because now he must worry about losing his job, his house, his car, all the accouterments that had been the measure of his corporate success. And as those concerns creep back in to control his psyche, he again becomes split personalities who can only agree on the desperate need for an escape from the emotional pain. Suicide becomes the acceptable choice. While holding the gun to his head, he hears the voice of his grandmother urging him on, saying, "*You might as well, you just another nigga now.*"[37] We are reminded here of Willy Loman's brother Ben who, in evaluating his brother's prospective suicide, calls it a "remarkable proposition." The twenty-thousand-dollar insurance policy is enough of a justification.

As with Ben, Covington's grandmother measures success in terms of material acquisitions. How the world sees you is the important concern. We observe in *Death of a Salesman* how Loman put so much value on business success that it literally drove him to suicide. Heller's Bob Slocum conveys the absurdity once again as, having fathomed very little in life to value, he ponders:

> What else will I have? My job? When I am fifty-five, I will have nothing more to look forward to than Arthur Baron's job and reaching sixty-five. When I am sixty-five, I will have nothing more to

look forward to than reaching seventy-five, or dying before then. And when I am seventy-five, I will have nothing more to look forward to than dying before eighty-five, or geriatric care in a nursing home.[38]

But even before Slocum, there was Sinclair Lewis's prototypical businessman George Babbitt who by age 48 had accepted his defeat in the battle against social conformity. "They've licked me; licked me to a finish!" he cried in mournful submission.

And yet, the dilemma — by the time we reach the point of Covington's life — has become even more exacerbated. When he decides to confront the system, he finds Haviland totally prepared. The CEO has arranged for Covington's own white secretary to press trumped up sexual harassment charges just in case the need should arise. In the face of such a threat, the once-heralded black executive resigns himself to an ignominious fate.

Loman had walked out into the garage to perform the task of asphyxiating himself. There to keep him company was the haunting figure of his brother Ben. Covington, in his grandmother, also has a conspiratorial relative. But along with that grandmother, Covington has the burden of more than one self. As the suicidal moment of truth arrives for him, he "turned the light on and made a mad dash down the basement steps, and there I was at the bottom, waiting for me."[39] In Covington's case it is not just a matter of one man killing himself, though that would be tragic enough. But in Covington's situation we have the added complexity of two men trying to kill one another, possessed of one body, never comprehending how the societally induced cataclysm could have ever been avoided.

Black Studies and the Academy: Ishmael Reed's Satire of College as Quasi-Corporation

Contemplating how he spent most of his time "on the phone assuaging people," Covington wondered in his journal addressed to Paul Walker whether that cousin had "anyone in the academic world analogous to the marketing professional."[1] Evidently, Walker worked at a college or university, perhaps as a professor. A college graduate himself, Covington was conscious of the postulated precept that college is a place where "academic freedom" is encouraged and respected. But what Covington might have been surprised to discover is that, especially in recent years, the college campus has taken on the appurtenances of a gigantic business enterprise where networking and making money reign as the predominant issues.

Ishmael Reed's novel *Japanese by Spring* provides us with a view of one college's hierarchical processes particularly as they pertain to black Professor Benjamin "Chappie" Puttbutt who calculates how he must compromise himself in order to get tenure. He had come to Jack London College with the understanding that after three years of teaching simultaneously in the English and Black Studies Departments, he would finally be given tenure in the Humanity Department, which propagates the tenets of Western civilization. That is where Puttbutt ultimately wants to be, and he engages in the process of virtually selling himself to those who will vote in his tenure decision. In pursuit of this objective he condemns affirmative action, declares that blacks "were lowering the standards" of the college, and even writes a book that he entitles *Blacks, America's Misfortune*.

For a while, Puttbutt's plan seems to be going quite well. He has appeased most of the members of the English Department as well as the chair of Women's Studies, Marsha Marx, who comes right out and tells him, "Don't worry about your job," an ambiguous imperative that nonetheless is reassuring for a man such as Puttbutt whose future is hanging so much in the balance. In this world of academic insanity, the Black Studies Department is a "satellite" of Women's Studies, and therein we begin to see the corporation-like mechanisms whereby the less respected entities are cast off together to do battle against each other, thereby decimating their limited resources to the point where neither has the wherewithal to withstand the assaults of their real institutional enemy.

In the back of his mind, Puttbutt has some concern about the rumor that an effort is being made to attract the black lesbian feminist poet, April Jokujoku. If hired, she will "kill" about five affirmative action "birds" with one "stone"; so Puttbutt is rightly concerned, but is then reassured, again by Marx who insists that the rumor "had no basis in fact." Still, true to the chameleon-like mode that has been a defining trait throughout his career, he proclaims his own feminism and

> memorized every mediocre line by Zora Neale Hurston. Could recite Sylvia Plath from memory. Could toss around terms like phallocentricity. Struggled to make sense of Catharine A. MacKinnon.[2]

He not only wants to stay in the good graces of the Women's Studies Department, but he also is cognizant of the fact that, though they are no longer a dominant force, the feminists in the Humanity Department continue to hold some sway and "he still had to be friends with them in case he needed their vote."[3] Absorbed in that dehumanizing process, he is reminiscent of Wade's Covington whose promotions were guaranteed by nothing less than self-deprecatory acts demanded by a ruthless superior.

Like Covington, Puttbutt seems not to have much of a choice. He wants job security and knows that in return he must pay a high price. When white students disrespect him — questioning his credentials and (as in the case of Robert Bass, Jr.) creating racist cartoons — he nonetheless feels compelled to defend their right to freedom of speech though he himself enjoys no such benefit. Far from being able to speak freely, he says what his superiors expect him to say to the point where he assesses black students' problems as being due to their own excessive demands and methods that are too confrontational. Having issued that declaration, Puttbutt's "colleagues in Humanity thought that he was so reasonable. So responsible."[4] As far as he can tell, "tenure was so close he could taste it."

Reed himself is no stranger to the tenure review process. In 1977, he was denied tenure at the University of California at Berkeley even though by that time he had published three incredible novels — *Yellow Back Radio Broke-Down, Mumbo Jumbo,* and *The Last Days of Louisiana Red.* He had published collections of poetry, and among his publishers were Doubleday and Random House. He submitted to his Department the stipulated number of letters from students, attesting to his teaching ability. And yet he still was denied. In an interview published a year later in *Shrovetide in Old New Orleans,* he explained some of the details of that fiasco. As it turns out, rather than being evaluated on the basis of academia-related criteria, he may have been judged on the basis of other things such as to whom he was married (a Semite), with whom he partied (not members of the English Department), and whether or not he was too "temperamental." Furthermore, it did not help matters that he had just recently formed an organization called The Before Columbus Foundation, a group whose aim was to "humble Judeo-Christian culture." One can just imagine how the nappy-headed, blue-jeaned, bearded Reed was perceived by Berkeley's English Department that at the time had no black full-time members.

It was, in Reed's words, "all part of a national trend." And Reed is wise enough to know that the tenure result that he experienced has been experienced by many other junior faculty members in academia who in some way or another are perceived as not "fitting in." In the *Shrovetide* interview, Reed reflects back on the tenure process, in which he was involved, and candidly concedes:

> I don't know many faculty people. Maybe they feel I haven't socialized with them. I don't attend their functions and social gatherings. Over the years I never attended those things. I'm busy. I'm not a party person.[5]

Contemplate, for a moment, that widely published author being invited to a wine-and-cheese party, and him saying bluntly, "I'm busy. I'm not a party person." Or maybe he was coy, begging off from the occasion, issuing his regrets at having made a previous commitment. Whichever of those possible responses is closer to having been the actual case, it certainly seems that Earl McClenney's book, about black survival in the office place, came out a decade too late for Reed and others like him who might have "benefited" from the stern admonition that "some parties you must go to for political reasons related to your job."[6] But then on the other hand, I rather doubt that McClenney's how-to book would have had any impact on Reed other than as the target for one of his vituperative satires.

In the July 14, 1995 issue of *The Chronicle of Higher Education*, another novelist/poet Jay Parini declared, "I would certainly advise all my younger colleagues who care about getting tenure to keep their mouths shut until the decision is made in their case."[7] That seems to be quite sound advice, especially considering how anything controversial that a candidate says will invariably be construed by some person or another as irreparably offensive.

Parini goes on to specify that "politics and ideology usually play a part" in tenure decisions. Reed's Puttbutt is so aware of this feature of the process that though he was a black power advocate when it was the trend in the 1960s, he changes over to become a "member of the growing anti-affirmative action industry," writing essays "about how your white colleagues don't respect you. About how you feel stigmatized. About how you feel inferior."[8] He is willing, for the moment, to ignore the fact that even without affirmative action, blacks as a whole are stigmatized and disrespected. But Puttbutt assumes he is safe, practically guaranteed tenure. As one of but a handful of black Ph.D.'s in the United States, he expects that his treatment will be better than what is afforded to blacks in general.

It is ironic that the fiercely independent Reed would acknowledge a certain kinship with a fictional character like Puttbutt. Yet, in a 1985 interview, the artist confirmed:

> For every Ishmael Reed there are hundreds of other talented black writers. I'm aware that I'm one of ... the tokens — a few of us have been picked out. There are many black writers who are very good but just don't get the publicity that prominent tokens get.[9]

There are those who will argue that such is the nature of the trade publishing industry. For every white person who gets a manuscript accepted, there are hundreds of other whites who get rejected.

But there is something more at stake when (as Reed calls them) the "East Coast intellectuals" have total power to determine which writers, and literary critics for that matter, will be allowed to define crucial issues such as the meaning of the Black Aesthetic. In an essay criticizing esteemed literary critic and former Modern Language Association president Houston A. Baker, Jr., Reed accuses, "They cherish the west, these 'real Black people,' and devote more references in the indexes of their books on the Black novel, to Mailer and Styron than to Black novelists and begin their books with a prayer to Plato."[10] Of course with the burgeoning schools of literary theory, it has become almost essential to include something about philosophers such as Kant and Heidegger or theorists such as Lacan, Bakhtin, and Derrida. As I mentioned earlier, the prospect looms great that blackness itself will consequently be defined in relationship to what whiteness means. Such literary analyses amount to what might properly be called the mediation of difference. Or, to phrase it a bit differently, we who are black and working in the academy may be contributing, more than we could ever have imagined, to the perpetuation of a status quo that in generations past made the study of black culture a tenuous endeavor.

Henry Louis Gates, Jr., in his theory-ladened text *Figures in Black*, borrows a term — "eclecticism" — that was used by Ralph Ellison who in a 1978 interview explained, "Anywhere I find a critic who has an idea or concept that seems useful, I grab it."[11] Gates is certainly not advocating that we all (black critics) make a mad dash to "white" theory. Rather, like Ellison, he advocates the use of whatever critic might assist us in explicating a primary text. If the critic that we discover just so happens to be white then so be it. The racial and cultural background of a potentially useful theorist should not be the determining factor.

And therein lies the crucial danger, for however beneficial, for example, Mikhail Bakhtin might be in deciphering the deeper meanings of Dostoevski, he will always fall short in the effort to uncover Richard Wright, however much the black writer may have been stylistically influenced by the 19th century Russian novelist. Baker understands what the shortcomings are as he censures Gates for believing "that literature is unrelated to culture. For culture consists in the interplay of various human symbolic systems, an interplay that is essential to the production and comprehension of meaning."[12] However one might wish to define the Black Aesthetic, it cannot be denied that it is inextricably linked to the singular circumstances that comprise the black experience, what the masses of blacks have been suffering since their arrival on American shores. It is that experience which best informs the black literary text, far better than any Eurocentric theorist could.

The only problem with Baker's criticism of Gates is that Baker himself often employs the strategy of borrowing perspectives and terminologies from Eurocentric theorists. We will recall Reed's scathing indictment. Elsewhere in the same essay, he labels Baker the "Humanities Colonial Secretary," a title meant to convey the sense in which, by employing his theoretical strategies, the distinguished black critic merely follows institutional orders. Sandra Adell, though significantly less abusive than Reed is in his criticism of Baker, nevertheless renders the same effect by characterizing what Baker does in criticizing Gates as "tantamount to the pot calling the kettle black." Using the two most highly regarded texts that have respectively been written by the two esteemed critics, she reveals the tragic flaw that, while not exactly making the texts irrelevant, does make us wonder which of two cultures is being exalted:

> While *Blues, Ideology, and Afro-American Literature* and *The Signifying Monkey* fall short of their emancipatory goal of freeing Afro-American literature from the hegemony of Eurocentric discourses, both studies bring into sharp relief what can best be described as a *nostalgia* for tradition. For to summon a tradition, for example, by reconstructing it, is to search for an authority, that of the tradition itself.... Something is always conserved; something always remains the Same.[13]

The tradition to which Adell refers is a white male literary tradition that had for centuries and even now continues to dictate the literary canon — which texts are to be revered, which texts are minor, which texts will be used in the classroom, and (saddest of all) even how the texts will be viewed in terms of their fundamental meanings. The addition of a multitude of Black Studies programs, even with their phenomenal stars, has not altered the relatively low status to which Afrocentricity has been relegated within the overall cultural hierarchy.

In *Japanese by Spring*, Reed renders us his own version of a Black Studies chairman, Charles Obi who, with his Harvard Ph.D., functions in essentially the same role as Naylor's second in command. He warns Puttbutt that "the liberals in the Humanity department say that you don't mix with them. How do you expect to get ahead if you're not collegial? Stroking people."[14] Perhaps Puttbutt simply is "not a party person," as the author has declared is his own disposition. But since his arrival at Jack London College, Puttbutt has been saying all the "right" things, working to make white people comfortable.

Obi's subtle threat is not so much different from what the supervisor in Heller's *Something Happened* enjoys reminding his subordinate: "You're not a free citizen as long as you're working for me." That perspective cuts against the grain of what a free society is supposed to represent. But then again, what becomes increasingly clear is that for most academicians, freedom does not exist in the de facto sense. And if freedom does not exist in the modern academy, then what are we to make of those claims for its existence in the world at large? In spite of the plethora of legal mechanisms, personal freedom is relative. One person's freedom ends where another's begins, and when that other is a work place superior, freedom is only a word.

Obi of course knows all this. He has been kowtowing longer than Puttbutt. He can keep Puttbutt waiting indefinitely and then lie when he does speak to him even about a matter so urgent as Puttbutt's employment contract. The chair makes Puttbutt wait for months. There is no sense of urgency on his part since he has already made Puttbutt promise to try and convince the Dean not to suspend Robert Bass, Jr., the white student who had been the perpetrator of so many racist acts on the campus grounds. Obi has fulfilled his role of second in command. He can callously move on to other things and, as the saying goes, leave Puttbutt to twist in the wind.

I recently attended a Henry Louis Gates lecture, after which a young black boy, sitting in the balcony, asked the scholar, "What do you do to help with the problems that blacks have in this country?" There was tension in the standing-room-only audience, and there were those who would have liked to have seen the boy removed if that had been possible. He could not have been any more than thirteen years old, brought to the lecture as part of a group wishing to expose him to a prominent black cultural event. But the boy must have, during the course of the lecture, become embroiled in an emotional dilemma. Seated as he was in the midst of this gathering, he could not forget where he had to return once the lecture was over. To his part of town. To his public school. To a world unaffected by the vast contributions being elaborated upon by the speaker to whom the boy was now listening.

Such social gaps have prompted Reed to note that "every poll I've read leads me to believe that there is a discrepancy between the political thought of real black people: and those opinions held by a handful of Christian-socialist intellectuals and professors crouching under the veil (ugh!) of the Black Christ and, most recently, the Black Lenin."[15] We can harken back to *Invisible Man* where Ellison himself uses "the veil" as a metaphor to emphasize the uncertainty with which we must regard the college founder who may or may not be facilitating black socioeconomic advancement. We know that Reed wants to "humble Judeo-Christian culture." He stresses that there exists a dichotomy between Afrocentric culture on one hand and Western culture on the other that has held dominance for so long that the former has been severely diluted and in some instances entirely appropriated.

It is to Gates's credit that he was able to quell the audience's whispering disapproval of the black boy's question. The scholar raised a hand — signaling his admirers to halt their mounting discontent — and said, "That's a good question." The boy, drawing on all his inner reserve, prepared to receive an answer which turned out to be something of a disappointment because while the boy was wondering about the nature of Gates's grassroots contributions, Gates could only offer the tenuous assertion, "I write." The audience was satisfied that this was enough of a social contribution, but the boy was not particularly impressed.

Reed disagrees with the Du Boisian notion that a talented tenth will lead the black masses out of their debilitating socioeconomic situations. In fact he has satirized that theory again and again in his various literary works. There is a professor in his novel *The Last Days of Louisiana Red* who teaches a course entitled "The Jaybird As An Omen In Afro-American Folklore." One wonders what the purpose of such a course would be for black college students, not to mention what the purpose would be for blacks outside the college milieu. In *The Free-Lance Pall-bearers*, a distinguished researcher is also the editor of *Studies on the Flank*, a journal that is detached from the reality of black life even as it purports to explain the essential factors affecting black people's lives. The researcher is a cold calculating observer who, even when physically in the black community, feels no personal connection to it. In conducting research, the exhilaration he feels is comparable to what many whites must have felt as they slummed Harlem's streets in the 1920s. He remarks:

> O, this is so thrilling! I even enjoyed the roughing up those kids gave me.... I'm working on a paper on the mores of segregated housing projects for the University of Chicago.... It enabled me to observe culturally deprived children at first hand.[16]

When asked what he means by "culturally deprived," the researcher replies that the children in housing projects "can't go to Lincoln

Center and devour Lilly Ponds," whereupon he is reminded that though fish eat "Lilly Ponds," such vegetation will hardly improve the lives of the disadvantaged children who are his research subjects. Such a diet in conjunction with a trip to Lincoln Center will accomplish about as much for blacks as the Black Studies programs at Harvard, Yale, and UPenn.

Reed makes it clear that the oppression suffered by blacks is not always due to an abusive white race. Blacks, particularly in academia, are quite capable of first exploiting and then ignoring the very blacks who were the source for their scholarly endeavors. Black Studies director Charles Obi was:

> always trying to be street. But his dress and style — busy — gave him away. Talked a lot of corny ghetto talk when he communicated with the brothers, but his stuff published in scholarly journals was unreadable.[17]

That characterization in *Japanese by Spring* echoes the following assessment rendered by Reed with regard to Houston Baker:

> I say enough of this hypocrisy of professors trying to be down, the middle class trying to drink Ripple and people flitting from one ideology to another ideology.... Be "real Black people?" Mr. Baker; you can start by learning how to make gumbo.[18]

According to Reed, Baker's professional posturing had evolved into an even larger illegitimacy as he allows himself to be hailed as the bringer of black cultural values.

Obi hails Puttbutt with the hearty greeting, "Hey, my brother." But Obi is not to be trusted. When he smiles at Puttbutt it "was one of two smiles that he owned." We will recall another HNIC, Ellison's Bledsoe, who can transpose his facial expressions in accordance with the particular occasion, that is in terms of whether or not he is conversing with a student or hobnobbing with an influential white patron. Likewise, Obi reserves his other smile for when he is "currying favor from higher-ups," the most prominent of whom is the president himself, Bright Stool, to whom Obi runs whenever he needs funds "to keep [his] department going."

Puttbutt will later condemn that relationship as a "neocolonial" arrangement. For the time being though, Stool regards Puttbutt with a certain degree of fondness also, calling him the "best affirmative action baby on campus" and praising his book as an unqualified "masterpiece." Indeed that president grows anxious wondering how the Department of Humanity could be taking so long to grant tenure to such a valuable human commodity.

As critical as Reed is of both Puttbutt and Obi, he saves his harshest satirical jabs for Stool whose name in itself alludes to the moral shortcoming. With his skillful "arbitraging methods"—tactics that were of such a questionable nature, in his former line of work, to have aroused the suspicions of the Securities and Exchange Commission—he now resides in a two-million-dollar mansion, has a lavish expense account, and a limousine at his disposal. All this he enjoys even as the rest of the college is straining for resources in the aftermath of a series of budget cuts.

We further learn that the president is a "refugee from the crash of '87." He is the fictional alter ego of Michael Milken, "junkbond king," who bilked the American public out of billions of dollars and precipitated a major Savings & Loan crisis, all the while reserving for himself yearly incomes that topped off at $550 million dollars a year.[19] The president is another Ivan Boesky, that famous trader in stocks who was so brazen as to hand-deliver his suitcases full of cash, payments for the information that it was against the law for him to have.

Wall Street analogies such as those are not as outlandish as at first might appear to be the case. As a foreign observer tells Puttbutt, "You Amerikans pay your executives too much money, that's part of the problem here."[20] In the instance of Milken, it was Drexel Burham Lambert, Inc. that allowed him his staggering salary, so outrageous in fact as to make it into *The Guiness Book of Records*. But even more alarming is the prospect that the record will soon be broken. In 1993, *Business Week* reported the top CEO salary at $127 million dollars, with the national average at almost $4 million.[21] What has allowed for those huge numbers is the recent trend toward giving executives stock options as well as other perks that can periodically be liquidated, expanding into totals that often dwarf the executive's own base salary. As far as the Board of Directors at Jack London College is concerned, Stool more than earns his keep in a position parallel to that of the corporate CEO. He "had been recruited" in the first place "in hopes that he could sell the university as well as he could sell stocks."[22]

College presidents themselves are quick to draw the comparison between themselves and private-sector CEOs. When asked about their salaries, most college presidents will vehemently declare that they are underpaid. Yet, Mark Rosenman, Vice President for Social Responsibility at the Union Institute, insists that the comparison between college presidents and corporate CEOs is entirely inappropriate. He emphasizes, in the May 5, 1993 issue of *The Chronicle of Higher Education*, that there exists a big difference between for-profit organizations and non-profit entities, the latter of which altruism should play a major part.

One would think that an institution of higher learning would be different than the typical large corporation. Rather than simply the "bottom line," academic freedom and liberal education should be accepted as predominant concerns. But as it turns out, broad-based education is not the priority at President Stool's institution.

> Another reason that the board of directors at Jack London had hired President Stool was because he vowed to put an end to capricious demands for a global university. The board believed that Jack London should be dedicated to the values of the West. Jack London's values.[23]

And thus we come to the issue of the source for the college's name, for in spite of his prodigious literary output, the writer Jack London was also an unabashed racist who looked upon China, with its enormous population, as a threat to Western civilization. Stereotyping the Korean as an inefficient coward, London went on, in an essay entitled "The Yellow Peril," to label the Japanese as unethical. The San Francisco born writer had but little more respect for the Chinese citizen other than to say that at least he is a hard worker. Of the Anglo-Saxon race, on the other hand, London declared "there is a certain integrity, a sternness of conscience, a melancholy responsibility of life, a sympathy and comradeship and warm human feel, which is ours, indubitably ours, and which we cannot teach to the Oriental."[24] In that same essay, London synopsized his praise for Anglo-Saxonism by stating succinctly, "We are a right-seeking race."

In "The Yellow Peril," London contended that there would not be so much to fear from China were it not for the "squatting" Japanese man eagerly awaiting the opportunity to "manage" the other. Equally revealing is London's "The Unparalleled Invasion," a futuristic allegory in which the Japanese put into effect their "management" technique until the Chinese banish them and then initiate their own brand of subtle expansionism. The Western world responds to the threat by implementing a plan of genocide in the form of germ warfare against the Chinese until they are finally exterminated. London applauded that result and detailed the sanitation procedures that followed, concluding that "it was a vast and happy intermingling of nationalities that settled down in China in 1982 and the years that followed.... We know today the splendid mechanical, intellectual, and art output that followed."[25] Appearing in 1914, in the essay collection *The Strength of the Strong*, that allegory concludes with the dominance of Western art and culture right there on the soil where Chinese culture once thrived.

So, Jack London College is meant to be a bastion of Western thought. The Miltonians (with their narrow-minded view of what good literature is) control the English Department. *Koons and Kikes* is a student-run newspaper reflecting the ideology that its name implies. And as for his part, Stool will not initiate change, especially as pertains to *Koons and Kikes* which draws its funding from powerful "right-wing corporations and law firms." That newspaper is Reed's satirization of the *Dartmouth Review* that in 1983, and then again in 1988, was unduly critical of a black professor's music course. The paper hurled epithets such as "intellectual farce" and "most outrageous gut course on campus." William Cole, the insulted teacher and as it turns out a close friend of Reed's, sued the newspaper, but that did not stop the proliferation of insulting statements, the most appalling of all focusing on Cole's physical appearance and characterizing him as unqualified even "to be a migrant fruitpicker."

In the novel, Stool ultimately must answer to the board of directors. But just as the actual president of Dartmouth had to be concerned about the fact that the *Review* has numerous prominent supporters, Stool cannot ignore the fact that Robert Bass, Sr., is the college's "biggest [financial] supporter" who brings with him a retinue of even more contributors who together form a quasi board of directors whose wishes Stool must always take into consideration.

The *Dartmouth Review* has as its number one principle that:

> Dartmouth's curriculum should stress the great ideas of Western civilization. The present symptoms of Dartmouth's curricular malaise are programs like women's studies, Afro-American studies, certain courses in the sociology and psychology department, Native American studies, and others.[26]

The *Review* has a strong impact in terms of influencing campus perspectives. One brave assistant professor of education, upon being interviewed by *The Chronicle of Higher Education*, lamented that "whole avenues of contemporary thought are not legitimate at Dartmouth."[27] Frightening indeed when one considers that this is our much heralded Ivy League, at an institution where of all places a "well-rounded liberal arts education" is supposed to occur.

In the Winter 1987 issue of *New Literary History*, a rather curious debate took place between three black scholars — Houston Baker, Henry Louis Gates, and the then up-and-coming Joyce Ann Joyce. Joyce is concerned about the theoretic direction that black literary criticism is taking and the "merger of Negro expression with Euro-American expression." And her concern is quite valid. For if such a "merger" of the cultures is taking place, it is inevitable that in our society, the Euro-American will continue to hold its place of dominance, defining the other and lessening the influence of those Reed refers to as the "real Black people," not necessarily the most literate but those who suffer most due to their darker color. Whether Western-oriented theorists can capture that pain, or even capture the essence of texts that explore the black agonies, remains a legitimate question. Or to use Audre Lorde's words, "What does it mean when the tools of a racist patriarchy are used to examine the fruits of that same patriarchy?"[28]

Rather than offer an in-depth exploration of that vital issue, Baker and Gates manned the garrisons (so to speak) from which they launched a barrage of vindictive comments aimed directly at Joyce. In response to her suggestion that black literary critics owed a duty to the black masses, Gates replied, "I do not think that my task as a critic is to lead black people to freedom."[29] That sounds strikingly similar to the "I write" response that he gave the black boy who asked what he did to help the black masses who are mired in social upheaval. Joyce would have us re-examine the efforts of W. E. B. Du Bois, Audre Lorde, Larry Neal, and Sonia Sanchez for examples of how black literary figures can "use their energies — in different ways — attempting to bring out the psychological and economic liberation of Black people."[30] What emerges finally in the debate, between Joyce on the one hand and Baker and Gates on the other, is the related vital question of who actually does benefit from the existence of Black Studies programs.

At Jack London College, Black Studies is an opportunity for football players to "get easy grades." This serves the president's purposes since it is important to keep athletes academically eligible. They are responsible for filling the college's coffers. And however much the admissions brochures talk about academics being a priority for student-athletes, they are, as Reed tells us, simply "meat on hooves" to be used for the purpose of "hauling in" the maximum load of money. That is what Black Studies means to Charles Obi who while working diligently "trying to be street" is also Stool's reliable lackey.

As Stool issues instructions to Vice President Witherspoon, we are further informed with regard to how much that president is opposed to academic diversity:

> Get me a list of those troublemakers who are behind this diversity movement. We'll chill them during the summer. Send them letters warning them not to come back. I need the names of some of their faculty supporters. Matata has sent me a list from inside his department. He's a team player. There's a nigger who can be trusted.[31]

Stool's first order of business is to appease those alumni who might withdraw their financial contributions if the college was to become diverted from its primary mission. He has a strategy for dealing with "recalcitrant" students and their professorial supporters, some of whom work in Black Studies. Obi of course is supportive of that mission as long as he can hold on to his academic fiefdom. Matata Musomi, "head of the Swahili contingent" is, in Stool's words, also a "team player" though Puttbutt will later be inclined to declare, with regard to those two Black Studies professors, that "if this were war you'd be hanged for treason."

Such is how Reed wants us to evaluate the academic malaise — as a war with concepts at stake that cut to the core of who we are as a free country, for who actually are the team players when the aim is to deny people their own individual opinions? When the term "team player" is used in the corporate setting, it refers to a willingness on the part of certain individuals to suspend their own beliefs for the survival and prosperity of the organization, the idea being that if the organization cannot prosper, then neither can individuals. But academia is supposed to be an entirely different realm where success should be measured by the extent to which divergent ideas are allowed to flourish. Jack London College is the antithesis of the free-thinking college community, and Black Studies in this setting merely lends its approval to the general administrative agenda.

It would seem that Black Studies would be at the vanguard of social change, and that Women's Studies programs would be valuable allies in the effort to make colleges something more than just factories pounding out a human product for the marketplace. In Reed's novel, the chair-woman of Women's Studies, Marsha Marx, urges Puttbutt to understand that "we should be on the same side. United in our fight against white male patriarchy and its control and manipulation of modes of produc-tion." But Marx becomes alliance-oriented only after a "mysterious Japan-ese group" buys the college and appoints Puttbutt "special assistant to the acting president," a Mr. Yamato who has replaced the ousted Stool. Putt-butt is promoted because he speaks Japanese, a language he had studied under Yamato himself. As Reed conveys, "Puttbutt figured that with Japanese under his belt he would adjust to the new realities of the com-ing postsettler era, a time when the domination of the United States by people of the same background would come to an end."[32]

Puttbutt anticipated the future quite well, for he now holds the posi-tion of second in command. He is the interpreter of administrative orders; and colleagues who earlier had refused even to acknowledge his presence, now smile longingly for the chance to be in his favor. Marx had previ-ously been brusque, aloof, and finally deceitful when it came to matters concerning Puttbutt's career. And for his part, as mentioned earlier, Putt-butt had only espoused feminist views for purposes of political correct-ness in order to appease certain members of the Humanity Department.

Women's Studies should receive the same respect that is afforded other more established academic disciplines. In her essay "Women's Studies as a Strategy for Change," sociologist Marcia Westkott declares that the mission is "to study the history of women, especially as it is recorded through the consciousness of women themselves.... Psyche and history are thus joined in the discovery of the ways that one's personal life has been shaped by being born a woman."[33] The conse-quences of having been born a woman, in a sexist society, should be of paramount concern to scholars as well as students who care about the prospects for social progress, just as Black Studies should serve as an important element in the battle to overcome racism. An alliance between the two programs would seem to be an inevitability.

However, another key factor is involved that pertains to how employees relate to one another when a powerful authority figure looms as a threat. Heller's Slocum best conveys this absurdity that is also the unavoidable reality:

> In the office in which I work there are five people of whom I am afraid. Each of these five people is afraid of four people (excluding

overlaps), for a total of twenty, and each of these twenty people is afraid of six people, making a total of one hundred and twenty people who are feared by at least one person. Each of these one hundred and twenty people is afraid of the other one hundred and nineteen.[34]

What seems to be paranoia is not paranoia at all, for those workers' fears are legitimate. Slocum himself winds up being assigned to replace Andy Kagle who is being punished for corporate improprieties such as disagreeing with his superiors, fraternizing with subordinates, and refusing to adhere to the company's unstated but firmly entrenched dress code. If Kagle can so easily be eliminated, then who among us has employment security?

College indeed should be different. But throbbing there beneath the surface of platitudes such as "free speech" and "academic freedom" is the pressure to eradicate tenure. One school, (the College of the Ozarks) that has already eliminated tenure, used the corporate world for its model. A trustee of the institution justifies the action by stipulating "there isn't any other business that I know of that grants lifetime employment."[35] While schools that abolish tenure may claim to be increasing faculty productivity, what actually is being accomplished is the institutionalization of fear — fear of disagreeing, fear of being different, fear even of associating (except in deferential ways) with those who have the power to destroy one's career.

Marx lied to Puttbutt when she told him that he did not have to worry about losing his job. The whole time she was assuring him he would get tenure, she was plotting behind the scenes to get Jokujoku to join the faculty. The black poet finally accepts an offer, agreeing to a $150,000-per-semester salary with perks that include a bodyguard, two secretaries, and a house in the mountains. Marx had actually been working hard, trying to make sure that Puttbutt would never get tenure. In that way more money would be available to meet Jokujoku's exorbitant demands. Yet Puttbutt is supposed to be utterly collegial, adhering to the tenets of altruistic teamwork even as the team grows less and less concerned about what his fate will be.

Puttbutt does not receive tenure. Indeed but for the Japanese takeover of the college, who knows where he would have wound up? Jokujoku, with her huge salary and accordant prestige, would have helped Women's Studies gain leverage in the battle for budgetary funding. It is the sort of leverage that Black Studies programs can suddenly achieve with the acquisition of faculty like Henry Louis Gates or Houston Baker. But I was somewhat startled when a colleague of mine recently referred to Black Studies at Harvard as not so much an academic discipline as Gates's own private industry, a corporate conglomerate in the midst of an academic world. Gates himself has postulated that "what our field needs is more entrepreneurs." Perhaps marginal programs in general could benefit to some degree from that approach.

Yet, even marginal programs should be concerned with much more than financial empowerment or, for that matter, interpretation of literature and the recapitulation of historical events. The mission should include, as Joyce declared in the case of Black Studies, an effort to "bring out the psychological and economic liberation of Black people." When the Japanese take over Jack London College, the academic curriculum is overhauled. The Department of Humanity is downsized to the point where it is now a mere branch of Ethnic Studies. Western Civilization that had previously consumed so much of undergraduate study has now been reduced to a simple European Studies program with a budget no greater than what had been afforded the Asian American, Native American, and Black Studies programs. Yamato had effected the change. But that is not the liberation to which Joyce had referred, for by the end of Reed's novel, what we are finally left with is the exchange of one oppressor for another, one "corporate" manager for another who is no more concerned about academic freedom than the former administration had been. And benefits, particularly for the masses of blacks in America, remain an unlikely prospect.

From Freelance Writer to Corporate Token: Jill Nelson's Volunteer Slavery

In recent years there has evolved a whole spate of books about what life has been like for blacks working at *The Washington Post*, that prominent newspaper second only to *The New York Times* in terms of journalistic prestige. In her autobiography *Laughing in the Dark*, Patrice Gaines for example recounts:

> I was involved in a complaint filed by the union against the *Post*.... About a year before the complaint, I had been put on a fast track for raises, to receive large increases in my salary every six months until I reached a pay comparable to my peers'. I had no idea I was making less than my coworkers. Then, after I had received two raises, a local magazine published an article showing a salary scale at the *Post* that listed me as the lowest paid female reporter.[1]

There are all sorts of excuses that such institutions can offer to justify such a discrepancy, rationales that declare criteria such as seniority and merit to be the reasons for disparity instead of race and sex discrimination. But according to Jill Nelson, a reporter with the *Post* during the late 1980s, that newspaper has been guilty of systemic discrimination through the years beginning at its inception in 1877. Citing statistics compiled in 1988 by the Baltimore-Washington Newspaper Guild, Nelson discloses that "black female reporters earned an average weekly salary of $791.33, white females $859.37, black males $920.46, and white males $988.68."[2] Black women earned only 80 percent of what their white male counterparts earned, and even black men and white women earned more than black women though the individuals in all those groups performed the same job tasks.

Matilda Butler and William Paisley, in their study *Women and the Mass Media*, place the blame for salary discrimination on the fact that "many male managers have stereotypic beliefs about the kinds of work that women can do and about the right of women to earn equal salaries.... Because men believe that women's income is secondary, they attempt to pay women less than men in the same positions."[3] In fact there has come in recent years to be a general consensus that sex-based discrimination occurs quite often in the corporate work place. In a 1994 Louis Harris poll, 500 top women executives were surveyed, and 33 percent noted "an unwillingness to give women equal compensation for equal work." An even larger number, 51 percent, of that group said there existed "a glass ceiling or a point beyond which women never seem to advance."[4]

That same year, the Women's Bureau of the Department of Labor conducted its own survey of more than 250,000 women, 65 percent of whom complained about salary inequity; 61 percent indicated that they had "little or no ability to advance." With regard to that latter complaint, the percentage increases to 69 percent and 70 percent for blue collar workers and technical workers respectively.[5] Such is the status of women in America's work force.

Nelson's story is confirmation that women have suffered greatly in the corporate work place. She characterizes her own situation thusly: "I'm a volunteer slave, a buppie. My price? A house, a Volvo, and the illusion of disposable income."[6] In 1986, she was hired to work on the staff of a magazine that the *Post* was in the process of initiating. Her salary was $50,000 which was significantly higher than the $33,000 Gaines was earning as a reporter for the *Metro* section; Gaines had started working there in 1985. But the *Post* had a special expectation of Nelson that in retrospect became clearer as she examined the cover of the magazine's first issue.

> The cover photograph is the face of a young black man, printed in dark browns and grays, fading first into shadow, then into black. The man looks threatening, furtive, hostile, and guilty: Richard Wright's fictional Bigger Thomas, who chopped up a white girl and stuffed her in the furnace, made real and transposed to the 1980s. The ultimate nightmare Negro.[7]

The caption for that cover page read, "Murder, Drugs, and the Rap Star," and what the *Post* seemed intent on doing was to portray black men in general in the most degrading manner possible, feeding, as

Nelson herself explains, "into white folks' stereotypes of young black men as inherently dangerous."[8] In a city where 75 percent of black men have encountered the criminal justice system and 50 percent, in some areas, are unemployed, it is not too difficult to see how the *Post* thought its ploy would be highly successful. Nor was their strategy a unique one. In the late 1800s and early 1900s, the author Thomas Dixon regularly characterized black men as lurking rapists from whom civilized white America needed protection. We saw in 1988 how effective it was for the Republicans to display the image of Willie Horton as if to personify all that was wrong with America. In the instance of O.J. Simpson, whether he is innocent or guilty, one has to wonder why it was exactly that his case received so much media attention. Was it due to his celebrity status? Or was it because a white woman was killed, a black man was accused, and somehow the message had to be gotten across along the lines of, "See, we told you how they are. We told you to leave them alone."

The *Post*'s first magazine issue was met head-on with a barrage of black citizen outrage. Led by radio station owner Cathy Hughes, organized protests were staged, including the strategy of blacks buying the Sunday newspaper and then appearing en masse at the steps of the *Post* to take out the magazine section and hurl it back at those *Post* offices. As an employee of the *Post*, Nelson felt caught in the middle, torn between allegiance to her colleagues at the newspaper and loyalty to D.C. blacks who were collectively harmed by the image reflected on the cover of the *Post*'s magazine. Earlier in the autobiography, Nelson declares that there is a "thin line between Uncle Tomming and Mau-Mauing.... On one side lies employment and self-hatred: on the other, the equally dubious honor of unemployment with integrity."[9] Those analogies might appear to be unduly extreme, to say that a working black person is an Uncle Tom, and one who is unemployed is a Mau-Mau warrior. But the symbolic reality of the situation is brought to bear as we consider how Nelson's "thin line" is no different than the "tightrope" that *Linden Hills*'s Smyth avers to Donnell as the place upon which they must spend their entire professional lives treading.

With Nelson's Mau-Mau/Uncle Tom characterization, we can perceive even further the corporate limitations of black identity. The author recalls how when she was first interviewed for a position at the *Post*, she felt as though she was being recruited "to join a crusade." But at the same time, as she puts it, "no one will tell me its objective." Why would someone (indeed someone quite intelligent) be recruited to participate in an important mission and then not be told what the mission was?

Perhaps the *Post* recruiters felt Nelson should have been grateful just for the opportunity to work at a prestigious newspaper. It was not for them to fill her in about every detail, about the deeper implications of her job situation. She should have been happy to go along with the program, be paid, and enjoy the fruits of established power as it offered her its smile of favoritism. That approach is not so different from what the slave Harriet Jacobs had to endure under the watchful eye of her owner Dr. Norcom who repeatedly propositioned her and then, when unsuccessful, reproached her with the admonition, "Did I not take you into the house, and make you the companion of my own children? ... Have I ever treated you like a negro?"[10] As far as that master was concerned, Jacobs should have been grateful not to have been treated "like a negro." Had she been treated like an ordinary "field Negro," the odds are that her life would have been even more miserable than it already was.

Norcom's imposition upon Jacobs was of a sexual nature, but that factor does not completely distinguish the slave victim's plight from Nelson's predicament since the abuse perpetrated by Nelson's supervisors rendered her as much in the throes of psychological bondage as had been the case with her nineteenth century predecessor. A friend of Nelson's, David Hardy who himself had been a *Post* employee, had tried his best to warn her:

> I don't give a goddamn how much they're paying you, it's not enough. They'll buy you and try to steal your soul, too.... Don't sell yourself cheap. Don't go to work there.[11]

While Hardy's language — with regard to buying and stealing and selling — might be construed as largely metaphorical, it would behoove us to examine the extent to which his words can be nonetheless taken quite literally. In hiring Nelson, what was it the *Post* sought to buy? And how much of herself was she willing to sell for the benefits that might accrue for her acceptance of certain conditions.

In further comparing Nelson with Jacobs, it is apropos to consider how close they are to having the same skin complexion. When I first read Jacobs's narrative in the late 1970s, I could not help but wonder what was it about Jacobs in particular that made Norcom willing to build her a house in the woods to facilitate his lewd objectives. It would be a full ten years later before I got my answer when I noticed on the cover of the Harvard edition that she was light-skinned enough to have passed for white if she had been so inclined. As one reads — especially in her "Sketches of Neighboring Slaveholders" chapter — about the horrors suffered by many blacks during slavery, it becomes abundantly clear that her circumstances were different from those suffered by other slaves who were flogged, scalded, and screwed down in gin machines, left there to be finally eaten by rats. In fact Norcom refused for quite some time to either hit Jacobs himself or allow anyone else to do so. She was, to use Malcolm X's words, a "house Negro," the "beneficiary" of life options unavailable to most other blacks.

The authors of *The Color Complex* maintain that the difference in terms of social acceptance between a light-skinned black woman and a dark-skinned black woman is as wide and distinct as the difference in acceptance between a white woman and a light-skinned black woman. Those authors further inform that:

> The ratio of difference in earnings between the light-skinned and the dark-skinned blacks was proportional to that between whites and blacks. For every 72 cents a dark-skinned black made, a light-skinned black earned a dollar. Even today, it appears that blacks with the lightest skin color have the best chances for success.... Drive past any inner-city housing project, and you cannot help but notice that the majority of residents are dark skinned. Even more disturbing, look behind the walls of the nation's prisons; they are filled with a disproportionate number of dark-skinned inmates.[12]

That assessment is useful in trying to understand the disparity in salaries between Nelson and Patrice Gaines. Gaines is darker than Nelson and was perhaps not as much valued or even trusted initially as the lighter-skinned black woman. As *The Color Complex* further conveys, even "blacks who are lower class but light skinned are more readily trusted by the general public, particularly by white employers."[13] That social phenomenon is so thoroughly imprinted upon the American psyche that it pervades every aspect of race-related interaction. It was what made the nineteenth century black writer Frances E. W. Harper portray her more affluent black characters as light-skinned; white readers could identify more with those characters and thereby have a basis to applaud, for example, the novel *Iola Leroy* as a whole. William Faulkner himself was not above believing that black men such as Ralph Bunche and Joe Louis were able to achieve only in proportion to the amount of white blood in their veins.

Nelson is keenly aware that light-skinned and dark-skinned blacks are perceived differently by the general American society. In analyzing her relationship with another light-skinned black woman writer, she confides, "Those with straight or pseudo-straight hair who are nearer light-skinned than dark, tend to grow up feeling we have something to prove — not just to white folks but to just about everyone."[14] The relationship that she has with that other writer, Thulani Davis, is tenuous at first as they "feel each other out" to determine the extent to which one or both of them may be "trading on [their] color to get over," whether they became "Eurocentric sell-outs" in the process of achieving success. Nelson and Davis finally reach a comfort zone of interaction, realizing that examining each other was "like looking in a mirror." The subtitle for Nelson's autobiography is "My Authentic Negro Experience" which would seem to raise a question concerning whether certain black experiences are more legitimate than others. But all are authentic in the sense that though different, they are the actual experiences of black people. "Authentic" would be a misappropriated term if the effort was to characterize the entire black race on the basis of one person's life. Fortunately, Nelson does not attempt this. However, as she raises the issue of authenticity, one hears the reverberating theme: Am I black enough? or has something been lost in an inculcation of mainstream societal values?

"When we were together," says Nelson of her relationship with Davis at an advanced stage, "our search for the authentic Negro experience was over: we were it."[15] As it turns out, Nelson's life experiences were quite similar to those of her light-complected friend, and they found a common ground for self-identification. But what happens to Nelson just outside the offices of the *Post* is another situation entirely. As enraged blacks conduct their demonstration against that first magazine issue, one black man tells her, "We're all still on the plantation." During that tumultuous period, Nelson had sought to remain incognito, slipping back and forth through the crowd on her way to and from work. But one day as she paused to listen, that man confronted her with the slavery analogy and, upon seeing her press pass, proceeded to berate her: "So you work for those racist dogs.... Just decided to stop off at the demonstration for the boss, huh?"[16] Telling her that if she is not part of the solution then she is part of the problem, he demands to know, "Which are you?" to which she responds, "I'm a black woman." But that is not enough for the stranger, and he rails back at her, "That don't mean shit if you work for the man.... Black is a state of mind, not the color of your skin.... What you gonna *do*? ... sit up there and collect your check."[17]

The test that that man in the crowd administers is significantly more difficult than what Nelson endured with her friend Thulani Davis, for what the author must now ponder is whether the earlier warning from her friend David Hardy has come to a tragic fruition. Has she really been bought in a process resembling the ante-bellum slave market where ownership dictated a slave's speech and actions? The stranger has caused her to contemplate whether she was hired in the first place just to be a "token spook," someone to be viewed as a "good, safe Negro by [her] colleagues." After three months at the *Post*, the only writing of hers that has been published is a short piece in the "grab-bag section" of the magazine. Having "integrated the staff, [she] needn't do much else." More than someone whose work would appear regularly in the magazine's pages, the *Post* evidently needed someone willing to give credence to the notion that things were improving as far as issues of race and gender were concerned. Publication was not as necessary as steadfast allegiance to the company. Her reward would be an income much higher than what other black women were earning during that time.

The year before her arrival at the *Post*, she had earned a mere $20,000 in New York City, working as a freelance writer. But in that capacity, she could choose her own topics and write from her own unique perspective. She wrote articles for *Essence*, *Ms.*, and *The Village Voice* before being recruited by the *Post* for its "crusade" about which, at the time of her hiring, she knew absolutely nothing.

In their essay "Race and Crime: The Role of the Media in Perpetuating Racism and Classism in America," researchers Ralph C. Gomes and Linda Faye Williams report that

> only about 4 percent of the reporters on daily newspapers are African Americans. Far fewer are editors and managers.... Compounding the problem of underrepresentation is the lack of knowledge of the African American community demonstrated by the present media intelligentsia. The lack of contact with African Americans and knowledge about African Americans on the part of white reporters and decision-makers in the media often leads to, at best, insensitivity when they report on the African American community and, at worst, "downright" racism.[18]

Those authors point out that the white-controlled media does not convey information objectively. The media instead reconstructs and interprets. If its writers are as ignorant about black life as Gomes and Williams suggest, then how can they either accurately or sensitively portray African Americans in the news? Race and class go a long way in determining which stories will be printed and how they are presented. For example, black street crime is given maximum attention while white-collar crimes go unnoticed. Whites are more likely to be depicted as victims while blacks are more often portrayed as victimizers. Rather than being a source to ameliorate America's sad racial dilemma, the media feeds on prejudice.

Instead of devoting the cover of the very first issue of the *Post* magazine to a black man who had been merely accused (later, he was found to be innocent) of a crime, why not devote the first cover story to something positive about the black community? With a black population as large as Washington D.C.'s, great things must be happening every day. But instead of highlighting a positive feature, the *Post* accentuated the negative. Once it discovered that a particular rap singer had recently been arrested, a dual purpose was put into effect. Not only could the magazine cover, with its ominous photo, feed into the stereotype of the black man as villain, the story itself could be shaped in such a way so as to render, as Nelson observes, the rap music art form as "fomenting racist insurrection." By taking this approach to reporting, the *Post* conformed to old methods of perpetuating racism and contributed to the method of polarization that characterizes current race relations.

As the protesters stand outside the *Post* building, their leader declares, "Sorry isn't enough!.... We want more. We want an issue of the magazine dedicated to us, to celebrating the positivity of beautiful black Washington!"[19] What immediately comes to my mind is that the Harlem Renaissance movement of the 1920s was substantially engineered by a Howard University professor. Moreover, gifted black writers such as Georgia Douglas Johnson, Jean Toomer, and Zora Neale Hurston made their homes in the nation's capital at certain crucial points in their lives. Each of those artists made vital contributions to that 1920s Renaissance era. Also, not nearly enough has been written about the D.C. organizations and library-sponsored events that influenced the Renaissance movement as much as anything else short of the goings-on in Harlem itself.

I have furthermore always been amazed at the impact that D.C.'s black educational institutions have had in a plethora of arenas throughout history. I think of Dunbar High School — formerly known as the Washington Colored High School until it was then named the "M"

Street School — with its incredible faculty that included the likes of nineteenth century theorist Anna Julia Cooper. I think of Howard University with its multitude of groundbreaking scholars, not the least of whom was E. Franklin Frazier, a noted sociologist not only in his own era but also in more modern times.

But how could the *Post*, with its overwhelmingly white staff, have had access to or, even with a notion, been interested in locating such information. When one considers how black history was first omitted and then only given token representation in formal classroom situations, it perhaps is not enough to say the *Post* should have gone back and done its homework. The problem that existed at the *Post* is endemic to practically all of America. Nathan McCall, another *Post* black reporter, conveys in his autobiography *Makes Me Wanna Holler* the nature of this social predicament. Having arrived at the newspaper in 1989, he remembers how

> the *Post* felt like a strange and alien world to me. Many of the people there, I learned, were silver-spoonish, trust-fund babies raised and educated in the insulated Ivy League. They were smart, but in a narrow, elitist way. They could expound at length about all kinds of esoterica, and they knew all there was to know about the intricacies of politics and people around the world. Yet they seemed to know nothing about blacks in the city where they lived and worked, or about those African Americans sitting in the newsroom next to them.[20]

McCall's observations parallel those of Gomes and Williams who concluded that such ignorance on the part of majority white newspaper staffs leads to "at best, insensitivity ... and at worst, 'downright' racism." As McCall characterizes the *Post* as a place that was "strange and alien," it brings to mind the *Star Trek* episode entitled "The Cage" where a spaceship full of humans crashes on an alien planet and the lone survivor is so mangled that the aliens must try to reconstruct her body. Only, they have no idea what she looked like originally, no model from which they can work. So what they recreate actually looks like a monster that resembles only vaguely who she once was.

That in essence is what has become of the black race in America, particularly as we have been portrayed by the media. We are stereotypes that were handed down through the generations. Continuing segregation has only fueled the vile flame of society's insidious ignorance. And yet some version of the news about blacks must be told.

As we consider the history of the media, with its limited depictions of blacks, one would think that by 1986, the *Post* would have given at least one African American enough rank within the organization to prevent mistakes such as the one made by its magazine. Actually, as Nelson informs us, there were two such blacks on the newspaper staff. But their function was, to say the least, quite dubious. As the protests are taking place, the author cannot help but wonder, "Where was Milton Coleman, assistant managing editor for Metro, the spook gatekeeper at the *Post*? Shouldn't he have picked up on the message the magazine was sending?"[21] The term "spook gatekeeper" is a reference to Sam Greenlee's novel *The Spook Who Sat by the Door* wherein it is uncertain whose interests the main character serves — the white organization for whom he works, African Americans in general, or a personal agenda that could be quite distinct from the interests of the other two groups. Patrice Gaines also makes note of Coleman's rather lofty position and expresses concern, at one point in her autobiography, over whether he can afford to be supportive of her in a situation that "might carry political ramifications for him in the corporate world in which he operated."[22] In my previous chapters, I have discussed at great length the issue of office politics. Tenuous circumstances, as Earl McClenney attested, become even more delicate when a person is either the only black or one of but a few blacks in a corporate setting. So Coleman, another one of those assistants to the assistant, must tread lightly in spite of the high-sounding position he holds.

And then there is Vincent Reed, "the *Post*'s H.N.I.C. (head Negro in charge) of community relations," who Nelson depicts during the protest as "standing by the floor-to-ceiling windows and looking down at the demonstrators."[23] He is yet another black who holds a highly visible position from which one might imagine that positive changes could be put into effect, but for the fact that he has no real power with which to do so. He is presumably the authority on how good relations can be arranged between the newspaper and the black community, but like Ellison's Bledsoe, he is content to wear a mask and pretend that all is well.

In assessing those administrators Coleman and Reed, other HNICs discussed earlier in this study immediately come to mind: Naylor's Maxwell Smyth; Xavier Donnell, and her self-absorbed second in command; Wade's William Covington; and Ishmael Reed's Benjamin Puttbutt and Charles Obi. Each of those men hold positions of quasi-authority where for their own survival they must adhere to a status quo to the point where little if anything is done to alter the conditions that make life so unbearable for the majority of blacks in America. Nelson reflects on what has become the prototypical syndrome:

> If the early 1970s were a time when many black people decided to "join the system and change it from within," by the late 1980s some of us have realized that the system isn't changing, we are — and not necessarily for the better.... it has become clear that the benefits of joining the system are limited and individual. A few people might be doing some good, but the race is just about where it had been.... most of us corporate Negroes aren't helping anyone but ourselves.[24]

As we consider the number of successful blacks who have given something back to their communities, it becomes rather obvious that what we have is a case of too little too late.

One question that arises from our analysis of Nelson concerns the extent to which she may be no better than those residents of Naylor's Linden Hills who measure racial progress in terms of their material acquisitions. She is proud of her salary and the fact that she can afford to buy a home and an expensive foreign car. Moreover, when her editor had shown her an advance copy of the first issue of the magazine, she was diplomatic in her response, saying, "I think the story's good, but not for the first issue." She tells us that what she really wanted to say was, "I think this looks horrible.... the photograph is ugly.... Is this really going to be the first issue of the magazine black folks in this city have so eagerly awaited?"[25] She had to "choose [her] words carefully" with colleagues all around "straining to hear [her] response." So, she declined to say anything that might cause her white associates to identify her with "the brother on the cover" even though, just like him, she is being used to help certain whites make a whole lot of money. In return she can bask in the knowledge that she is a black person who has been accepted. All is indeed well until, like Johnson's ex-coloured man, she conducts the deeper search for her life's purpose and becomes rather disturbed by what she ultimately finds.

Plunging into a state of severe depression, she thinks back to "the picture taken a few weeks earlier of the magazine staff in front of the Jefferson Memorial, which is scheduled to run in the third issue. I sit front row center, grinning like a latter day Sally Hemings, Jefferson's black mistress. Oh yassuh, boss, I'm just a happy darkie."[26] Here again we have the slavery analogy, this time in the form of Thomas Jefferson, the third president who himself was a slaveowner even as he helped construct the *Declaration of Independence*, which professed the "unalienable right" of every man to be free. As if the denial of freedom to the black race was not enough, he displayed his hypocrisy even further by engaging in a sexual liaison with Hemings who was a member of that so-called inferior group. That was the height of hypocrisy. Studying the photo, Nelson now fathoms how her role in a yet more modern conspiracy has helped to perpetuate conditions of black subjugation.

Her emotional slump is accompanied by a physical regression so profound that even on Saturday nights, she is "stressed to the max, exhausted." The only phone calls she gets are ones where fellow blacks vent their considerable outrage against what the magazine that she works for has done. In response, she overindulges in dangerous habits, eating and drinking and smoking excessively, developing, as she tells us, "what feels like a permanent knot in my stomach." She has just about lost all control.

In a last-ditch effort to reverse her decline, she approaches Jay Lovinger, the editor most responsible for recruiting her to the *Post* in the first place. She tells him about her difficulties at the magazine, how little of her work is being used, and how little respect she receives from her immediate supervisor, the editor Amanda Spake. But even as she complains, she has to stop in mid-sentence because the expression on Lovinger's face betrays how he is no longer comfortable with her, how indeed he is "slightly intimidated." I have already discussed how important it is for blacks to make white supervisors feel comfortable. That is why Puttbutt opposed affirmative action, why Covington allowed Haviland to question his wife's parental background. Nelson, however, by filing her complaint, violates the unspoken rule.

As his discomfort increases, the editor seeks escape from the increasingly awkward situation and urges Nelson to discuss the matter with Milton Coleman, the black executive that she has already told us is the newspaper's "spook gatekeeper." She applies diplomacy and tells him "okay," pretending that indeed she will talk it over with the assistant managing editor. Actually though, she does no such thing, preferring instead to "challenge the patriarchal model," a phrase used by anthropologist Leith Mullings in explaining how "ideologies that stigmatize women of color have been central to maintaining class, race, and gender inequality."[27] Those ideologies, says Mullings, include the perception that women of color will be superwomen, matriarchs, children, or mammies. An independent-minded black woman breaking out of those categories can find herself wreaking havoc with a white supervisor's equilibrium.

Lovinger offers Nelson the further option of going back and trying to work things out with Spake, whereupon Nelson arranges a meeting immediately but, once she arrives, finds her on the telephone, complaining to "someone." After hanging up the phone, Spake is strangely brusque. When Nelson suggests that they get a cup of coffee, Spake retorts, "I don't drink coffee." When she tells her that Lovinger wants to print an article on Oprah Winfrey, Spake snaps back, "Do you want me to be your editor?" Nelson is able to maintain her composure and tells this supervisor, "I feel you're about the best editor available." Spake, still rude, simply responds, "Well, you damn well better act like it." That supervisor conforms to the pattern we saw exemplified in Bob Slocum's boss who insultingly proclaimed, "You're a grown-up man" but "you do have to stand there and take it."

Reflecting back on that encounter with Spake, Nelson confesses that she did seriously "contemplate smacking her." Yet virtually the same purpose had been accomplished when she reported her discontent to Amanda's supervisor. It had probably been Lovinger with whom Spake was talking on the phone when Nelson arrived for her attempt at reconciliation. One senses that an alliance of sorts was being forged between the two white supervisors suddenly faced with a disgruntled black employee. With one supervisor uncomfortable and the other enraged, Nelson's journalistic future was indeed becoming quite bleak.

In *Japanese by Spring* we were presented with the issue of whether or not black men and white women were "in the same boat" as far as being victims of oppression was concerned. But then we learned that Marsha Marx, chairwoman of Women's Studies, was actually competing against Puttbutt to gain favor with the corrupt Bright Stool administration. And Puttbutt espoused feminism only for the purpose of facilitating his quest for tenure. As between Marx and Puttbutt there was no relationship of trust, no alliance of oppressed individuals.

Having examined the *Post*'s history of gender and race discrimination and considered the failure of an alliance between black men and white women, what are the prospects of an alliance between the women of those two races? Harriet Jacobs's slave narrative is instructive and indeed serves as a precedent upon which we may base our conclusions about black and white women in contemporary times. Suspecting that her husband has been tormenting Jacobs, Mrs. Norcom orders that slave to tell her everything. And when Jacobs does as she is ordered, giving

Mrs. Norcom the details of her husband's impositions, the slavemaster's wife

> wept, and sometimes groaned. She spoke in tones so sad, that I was touched by her grief. The tears came to my eyes; but I was soon convinced that her emotions arose from anger and wounded pride.... she had no compassion for the poor victim of her husband's perfidy. She pitied herself as a martyr; but she was incapable of feeling for the condition of shame and misery in which her unfortunate, helpless slave was placed.[28]

Dr. Norcom had had numerous affairs with the slaves of his plantation, selling them off as they became threats to his home's tranquillity. What was it that kept Mrs. Norcom from identifying with the abuse that they all, as women, had been subjected to both at the hands of her husband and the overall slave system? The feminist bell hooks contends that "if the white woman struggled to change the lot of the black slave woman, her own social position on the race-sex hierarchy would be altered."[29] Now even as slavery is only an afterthought for many Americans, the dynamics of that centuries long institution remain paradoxically intact. Women are victimized by sex discrimination, but white women have the advantage of skin color. They are at least one rung above the black woman and must be concerned about jeopardizing their relatively privileged position.

As with most organizations, the *Post* had a method of showing favoritism to particular members of its staff. "Virtually no one is fired," says Nelson. But of course there are other ways that an entrenched system can vent its hostility against those who are not considered part of "the team." These outcasts, says Nelson, are "the hopeless" who "are simply paid regularly and ignored. Their bylines seldom appear in the paper.... virtually immovable masses of reporter-matter that arrived full of talent, eagerness, hope, and promise and then either weren't chosen, weren't lucky, or couldn't hack cutting throats."[30] Such could very easily be the fate of any number of individuals regardless of their race, but as Nelson explains, for "black folks" it amounts to a "journalistic purgatory" in which the "rules are changed" to keep them in permanent check.

And then there was the case of black woman reporter Janet Cooke who concocted the story about an eight-year-old heroin addict and turned it into a series of articles that won her the Pulitzer Prize. Once it became known that it was all just a hoax, she was forced to resign and return the prestigious award. Nelson talks about how "the Janet Cooke affair has been infamous in journalistic circles ever since."[31] I can attest that the tragedy of Janet Cooke's situation reverberated far beyond journalistic circles. When I first arrived at the University of Toledo in 1985, she was the talk of the campus. One professor who taught her as an undergraduate characterized her as a go-getter and confided to me that he was not at all surprised at her transgression. Since I was a mere instructor at the time and he was a white full professor, I did not pursue the deeper meaning behind what I now can say was his view that such is to be expected of certain black people.

What Nelson wants us to consider (and what my then senior colleague perhaps did not so much care to understand) is "why" Cooke did what she did. It is a quite telling commentary on the American state of affairs that in describing Cooke's efforts to advance in the corporate setting, Nelson must point to the fact that she was "pretty" and had "long hair." She "socialized primarily with white people" and would have done virtually anything "to succeed on white men's terms." In other words, she was willing to take on the role of lackey even if it meant perpetuating the myth of blacks as decadent and unworthy of the social equality for which we have been fighting so long. To construct the image of an eight-year-old boy whose mother's boyfriend "shoots him up" was as much an effort at perpetuating racist stereotypes as what the magazine editor did in her subtle characterization of the black rap star as an innately dangerous creature. The only difference it would seem between the two employees is that while one held disdain for blacks in general, the other one hated herself.

Cooke's frame of mind is a psychological state that Nelson seeks desperately to avoid. Having gone over her supervisor's head, she has "to make the best of a bad situation, to fit in without selling out, becoming a Tonto or a Samuel Pierce (the head of HUD under Reagan)."[32] But how is it possible to survive emotionally, caught thus between the two worlds? Applying yet again the slavery analogy, Nelson invokes the imagery of Nat Turner on one hand and "Mammy" on the other. Earlier she had spoken about how life for blacks in America "does tend to make some of us crazy." Mammy will survive with her nurturing self-effacing pose while Turner is perfunctorily executed. Nelson goes to great lengths to say that she is not Mammy, but rather "may be part of Nat Turner's gang." She opposes the system and advocates structural change.

Needless to say, with such an attitude, she will not be able to fit into this corporate milieu, and her fate is certainly sealed at the point where she is elected unit chairperson of a local newspaper union that is in the midst of filing yet another grievance. Regardless of her journalistic talents, she is destined to be banished into the realm of those "hopeless" reporters who are simply paid, ignored, and forgotten. But her editors must be careful how they assess her development, or alleged lack thereof, in the formal evaluative process. Having spent almost two years trying to get her first six-month evaluation, she is finally evaluated two weeks after her election. That evaluation in part read:

> Mutual trust — I don't think she feels we have her best interests at heart, and she sometimes seems to have her own agenda. The problem is that she may not be getting all she can in the way of growth from the editing process and we may not be getting the special things she has to give. There are also racial and sexual sensitivities — and now, with her union position — management vs. worker sensitivities.[33]

Earl McClenney, in his *How to Survive* book, warns that blacks in the corporate setting should be concerned when "words are not precise and clear" on their evaluations, when everything becomes subjective. That how-to expert further concludes that "whites have some funny notions of loyalty and cooperativeness when it comes to blacks."[34] Those funny notions to which McClenney refers are part and parcel of the white supremacist theory that blacks ought to be grateful for the jobs that they get, should readily accept the opportunity to do what they are told. Or in the case of Nelson, she should have understood what the *Post*'s agenda was in terms of its coverage of African Americans. Her responsibility, as perceived by her supervisors, was to just be a faithful foot soldier.

Having, in the minds of her superiors, thus abdicated her "responsibility," she now is accused of being untrustworthy, pursuing an agenda out of line with her employer's "crusade." Indeed the two agendas are different. While the newspaper was inclined to depict blacks as the pathological products of a deviant culture, Nelson sought to accentuate the positive. As a consequence of her complaint to Lovinger, she is assigned a new editor, Jeanne McManus, who also is "brusque, condescending, and whiny." Nelson is right back where she started, fighting to get her Oprah Winfrey story into print, and fighting now also for her story about attorney Alton Maddox who was then representing several young black men who had been chased out of Howard Beach because it was presumed that they were there to visit a white girl. Actually, the young men were there to look into the purchase of a car. Still they were chased, one out onto a highway where he was struck by a car and killed. Nelson does wind up getting that story published, but the fight to do so leaves a "bitter taste in [her] mouth," and she plunges even further from grace with the powers that be at the *Post*.

Not surprisingly, she is finally transferred from the magazine staff to the Metropolitan Desk, also known as the "race riot beat," since during the 1960s, most white reporters were afraid to go to the riot sites, so blacks were recruited for that particular purpose. And the Metro Desk is still the department where most of the black reporters are found. For Nelson, however, the transfer amounts to a descent into hell where her new supervisor's mission is to "cut [her] down to size." In his mind she is little more than a "childlike native" who will on occasion have to be "bullwhipped." One of her first assignments is to write "a story about fear of D.C. in academia." But upon interviewing students, she finds that none of them are frightened about where they live. Nelson conveys this information to her new supervisor who then tells her to call the students' parents to find out if they are afraid *for* their children. Nelson refuses to perform this task, rejecting the idea as

> absurd.... You want me to call up someone's mother in Colorado and say what? "Hello, I'm a reporter for *The Washington Post* and I'm just calling to find out if you're worried because Suzie is at school in the nation's homicide capital." Are you kidding? Even if she wasn't worried, she would be after my phone call. I won't do it.[35]

The supervisor argues, "You can't just refuse to do what an editor wants," whereupon Nelson responds angrily, "It's creating news, creating an issue. It offends my sense of journalistic integrity.... my sense of personal integrity."[36] Located now in a new department, she is yet again forced to do battle against the pervasive stereotypes. "It was," she says, "shocking to some of us to realize that journalism is, first and foremost, a business: its first responsibility is not to the truth, or even to readers, but to corporate America."[37] Corporate America of course has always been lacking in terms of how it perceives black America, and in urging its images onto the public, it is as culpable as any other entity for our current social malaise.

In spite of Nelson having a "plateful of feature stories in the works already," her new supervisor "delighted" in sending her out on daily assignments that were "scarcely newsworthy." And then came the drug trial of Marion Barry when Nelson reluctantly agrees "to become the spook who sits in court." She accordingly is assigned to a five-person team; the other reporters are white. As the trial proceeds, Nelson attends daily staff meetings where plans are made for the next day's story. But instead of being a primary reporter, she finds herself once again cast in the role of a token. If the black community persists in its charge that the *Post* is a racist organization, the editors "can point their fingers at me and retort, 'How are we racist? Jill Nelson was on the trial team and everyone knows she's pro-black.'"[38] Meanwhile her perspectives on the case are not published and though colleagues listen politely in the meetings, they "do what they planned anyway."

Nelson nevertheless works diligently on the Marion Barry story and submits an article that finally garners praise from her supervisor who declares, "It's a really good story." But when Nelson sees it in print it is buried deep in the "Style" section with the minimizing title, "After the Verdict, Food for Thought." Color commentary? News direct from the Mau-Mau front? Driven to tears, she can barely make it home before she goes "crazy softly, silently." She is now like Bill Covington, fading into a realm of insanity with "different voices in [her] head screaming for dominance." Such is the price she has paid for a job that she once felt held so much promise. And the process of emotionally healing herself begins only when she tenders her resignation.

Our Pathological Inheritance: "Sex and Racism" in Bebe Moore Campbell's Brothers and Sisters

In *The Signifying Monkey*, Henry Louis Gates asserts "that all texts signify upon other texts, in motivated and unmotivated ways."[1] By "signifying," he means that texts have a tendency to reflect upon the ideas of previously written texts. Explaining further this theory of intertextuality, he stipulates that later texts "talk to" earlier texts in what amounts to an ongoing process of author-to-author revision. According to Gates, the beginnings of this technique can be traced back to the Yoruba trickster figure Esu-Elegbara who in African mythology "interprets the will of the gods to man." In spite of the trickster's predisposition for ambiguity, disruption, and open-endedness, he nevertheless serves as translator for an oral tradition that is a hallmark of African culture.

Gates explains how the tradition continued with the advent of slavery in America to the point where slaves who had escaped would, when reconstructing their lives in literary form, employ the same techniques and themes that had been used by other slaves in their facilitation of an oral tradition. Gates realizes that, as time has passed, "in general, black authors do not admit to a line of literary descent within their own literary tradition."[2] But whether they admit it or not, the evidence exists for this particular tradition, forming in essence what Gates refers to as "the language of the tradition, employing its tropes, its rhetorical strategies, and its ostensible subject matter, the so-called Black Experience."[3] So, for example, we are made to look anew at *Invisible Man* and ponder the extent to which that novel is a reflection of what Ellison detected in the work of his mentor Richard Wright, particularly as pertains to *Native Son*. And we must reexamine *The Color Purple* for the evidence of how it is to a large extent Walker's response to Zora Neale Hurston's *Their Eyes Were Watching God*.

One wonders, however, if that theory of transference can pass muster in an instance where the novelist signifies not upon another novel or even upon what might be considered literature in the strict sense, but instead upon a sociological treatise. What I am suggesting is that in writing her novel *Brothers and Sisters*, Bebe Moore Campbell relied substantially on Calvin Hernton's *Sex and Racism in America* for the thematic underpinnings of what she would develop into a full-blown portrayal of how racism has effected human sexuality to such a degree that most Americans exist in a state of pathological flux.

In a manner similar to that of Jill Nelson, Campbell originally did freelance work for magazines such as *Ebony* and *Essence* within whose pages an optimistic style of writing is almost as important as factual data. In "Polishing Your Business Image," which appeared in the March, 1984 issue of *Essence*, Campbell stresses the importance of "dressing, team-playing and networking," and she advises that "the people who see their goals to fruition can hang tough…. Part of making it in business means promoting an image that mirrors the internal one that says: There's no stopping me."[4] We have already learned, however, from earlier chapters in this study that the situation for African Americans is actually somewhat more complicated. Hanging tough can be fairly impossible when the image that must be projected bears little resemblance to who a person actually is.

Other such articles by Campbell include "Success Beyond the Open Door" in the August, 1990 issue of *Black Enterprise*, and the previously mentioned "Blacks Who Live in a White World" (*Ebony*, March, 1982) where she assures us that black managers "are not abandoning their roots." Rather, says Campbell, "most feel strongly about keeping their blackness intact and, after a while, they begin to understand how to do that for who they are, and where they are a lot better than they did at the beginning of their careers. They don't cross over."[5] That statement is so convoluted and vague as to be almost incomprehensible. The author contends that blacks who work in white corporations keep their blackness because they "understand how to do it for who they are." But that is exactly my question: Who are we once we have been subjected to white indoctrination? *How* are we better off emotionally than we were "at the beginning of [our] careers?"

In her July, 1987 *Ebony* article entitled "Is It True What They Say About Black Men?," Campbell analyzes yet another provocative issue. Most Americans are familiar with the array of stereotypes concerning black men, stereotypes handed down through the centuries that allege sexual prowess, lower intelligence, and overall moral inadequacy. Campbell's goal in writing her essay was to refute those prevailing stereotypes and replace them with evidence of black male accomplishment. To that end, she offers evidence such as *Black Enterprise*'s list of top 100 black businesses, and among other things, she cites black psychiatrist Price M. Cobbs who asserts that in the 1960s, fewer than 20 percent of black children grew up in single-parent homes. On the issue of a perceived preference of black men for white women, Campbell pointed to U.S. Census Bureau data which revealed that from 1980 to 1984, there was actually a decline in the number of black men and white women marrying one another, down from 122,000 in 1980 to 110,000 in 1984. In that article, Campbell concludes her defense of black men by stressing that inequities we have suffered regarding unemployment, incarceration, and relatively early death have not prevented some of us from winning Nobel Peace Prizes, Oscar awards, gold medals, and platinum records. Laudable accomplishments indeed, that is until one adds up the number of blacks who have actually won Oscars and Nobel Prizes. And Olympic gold medals and platinum records are as much used to reinforce stereotypes as they are used to convey blacks' ability.

What becomes obvious when studying Campbell's articles in popular periodicals is that she has been prone to manipulate statistics in such a way as to support her position even in the face of ample evidence that would tend to support a different view. For example, in the July, 1987 *Ebony* article, she limited herself to data collected from 1980 to 1984, to draw the conclusion that black men are becoming less interested in marrying white women. However, as her forum becomes more "literary," so does Campbell's approach to analyzing the problem become appropriately complex as in an essay she contributed to Marita Golden's anthology *Wild Women Don't Wear No Blues: Black Women Writers on Love, Men, and Sex*. At the beginning of her essay "Black Men, White Women: A Sister Relinquishes Her Anger," Campbell presents us with the following anecdote:

> Two wealthy black businessmen are strolling down the street and one says to the other, "Man, let's try to get a date with the next white women we see." His friend agrees and soon they notice two white women approaching them. One is young and pretty; the other is over seventy, not very attractive, and has difficulty walking. One of the men says quickly, "I want the old one." His amazed companion asks, "Why in the world do you prefer her?"
> "Because she's been white longer."[6]

Of course that story is an exaggeration of what Campbell now accepts as a crucial psychological phenomenon. Nonetheless her anecdote makes the point quite effectively that many black men have been brainwashed into loving white skin. Instead of using the relatively short four-year span of statistics that she had used for her 1987 *Ebony* article, she now uses statistics covering an 18-year period to render an argument entirely contrary to what she had argued before. According to the Census Bureau, while in 1970 there were 41,000 interracial couples where the husband was black and the wife was white, by 1988, the number had increased to 149,000. As Campbell herself points out, that total still represents only a small percentage of black men, less than four per cent actually. But in her anthology essay, she has reversed her position of defending black men and instead subtly urged that black women should be concerned since "in a drought, even one drop of water is missed."

Having abandoned her earlier notion that interracial marriage is becoming less and less of a problem, Campbell goes on in her novel *Brothers and Sisters* to explore in great depth the sexual consequences of life in a racist society. Black Yale graduate Humphrey Boone has just been hired as senior vice president of Angel City National Bank in Los Angeles; he was told while being interviewed that in five years he will become the bank president. Of Boone's habits, we learn that his showers last "exactly thirty minutes" and "nothing was out of place" because "he hated the sight of disorder." That meticulousness reminds us of Naylor's Maxwell Smyth. But it is only upon learning that Boone's "hair was very kinky" and it "offended him" that we begin to comprehend an inferiority complex along the lines of what the author Richard Wright depicted in *Lawd Today* where black postal worker Jake Jackson "surveyed the unruly strands with the apprehensive air of a veteran field marshal inspecting the fortifications and wire-entanglements of an alien army."[7] Unruly was the way Jackson perceived his own hair and he used one military metaphor after another to depict his struggle against it including "the most powerful weapon at his command.... a pink jar of hair pomade labeled, LAY 'EM LOW."[8] The battle continued in what was for him a daily ritual culminating in the command to his wife, "GET ME A STOCKING CAP!" The unruly strands were subdued, made to lie down in orderly fashion; he was suitable now to venture out into the public.

For a period of time between the late 1960s and the mid–1970s, many blacks in America delighted in wearing large "Afro" hairstyles. Prior to that time, hair straightening or "conking" (as Malcolm X refers to it in his autobiography) was generally accepted as the way to maintain a desirable appearance. "Do-rags" and "mammy-leg" caps were necessary pieces of equipment. The "black is beautiful" era was a brief respite from the traditional degrading methods of altering our appearance, but by the late 1970s, we were right back where we started, battling our naps, in some way or another, in the effort to emulate whiteness.

Set in the early 1990s, *Brothers and Sisters* reveals that a decade and a half after the "black is beautiful" era, circumstances have reverted back to the pre-1960s condition. Also working at Angel City National Bank is 34-year-old regional operations manager Esther Jackson who is dark-skinned and heavy-breasted with "a behind that jutted out into a rounded curve." She is intelligent, ambitious, and wants to advance into the world of commercial lending. Boone could help her but she is not his main priority.

Instead his interests are drawn to Mallory Post, a blond commercial lender whose "nose and lips were thin" and whose "skin was the palest of ivory." In *Sex and Racism in America*, Hernton talks about the "myth of white womanhood" and how its perpetuation has "elevated" white women to the "status of a near goddess." It is the same phenomenon to which Barbara Welter refers in *Dimity Convictions* as she talks about the "cult of true womanhood," that widespread perception of white women in nineteenth-century America. Under the rubric of that code, women were supposed to be domestic, submissive, pious, and pure. Women's magazines, gift annuals, and religious literature of the period reinforced the perception that this was how a woman should be. The black woman of course was involuntarily exempted since the era of slavery and its subsequent decades made being a lady, especially in public, virtually an impossibility.

It is the *public* image that is so crucial. Just as Welter emphasizes the significance of reinforcement from the literature of that era, Hernton specifies how "the mass media, newspapers, magazines, radio, and especially television" now make it "all but impossible for the black man to separate his view of the *ideal* woman from that of the *white* woman."[9] It does not matter that in private trysts, the black woman has been valued for her sexuality, because unless she is publicly acknowledged, what goes on behind closed doors affords her no more than what she had in the days when she could be randomly assaulted by anyone. When Boone looks at Jackson,

> he couldn't help but compare [her] to other women, women who were pale and quiet and pretty. Women who smiled at him from big

screens and small screens and magazine covers. They were always welcoming, with their dazzling white smiles.... This was the type of woman he needed sitting next to him in his Mercedes when the top was down. This was the kind of woman, as flashy as a bar of gold, whose streaming hair let everyone know that he was important, that he was somebody.[10]

That vice president is in search of a status symbol. Bill Covington had been satisfied to marry a light-skinned black woman. But Naylor's Smyth and Donnell are biding their time in hopes of garnering a greater prize. There is a certain amount of danger involved as many in white America are still adamantly opposed to interracial unions. Many in black America likewise are appalled when one of their own crosses over to date or marry a white person.

But, as Hernton tells us, it is this sense of danger that may actually enhance the value of the white woman as prize. Says Hernton, "The perils and sacrifices of associating with a white woman may tend to enhance her value in the eyes of the black man. To such a black man, the prize is worth the challenge."[11] The longtime taboo against black man/white woman interracial relationships has served to make the two parties yet more attractive to one another.

Hernton's brutally honest appraisal of the situation first appeared in 1965, and some may be inclined to argue that things have changed considerably since then. Others contend that as far as this particular issue is concerned, nothing has changed at all. Writing 22 years later, Earl McClenney has a chapter devoted exclusively to "White Women" where he succinctly advises, "Don't mess with them. Leave these broads alone, especially where you work."[12] While McClenney does come across as both a racist and a sexist — discouraging all relationships between black men and white women, and referring to white women as "broads" — he is writing in the vernacular of that somewhat homogeneous group known as black male Americans. When he summarily instructs us not to "mess with" white women, he is invoking the language of thousands of southern black mothers who, throughout the generations, issued this warning to their young male children: "Stay away from white women!" Those old black women understood the emotional pull that the white woman had on black boys who all their lives had been bombarded with the predominant image of white female beauty. And yet white men declared white women off-limits. Black mothers responded as best they could in the effort to save their sons' lives.

As is typical of his practical writing style, McClenney warns black men, who are isolated in a white corporate setting, to "remember Emmett Till." Now this might sound like an outdated approach when one thinks of black survival in the office place. Till was the 14-year-old Chicagoan who was visiting relatives near Money, Mississippi, during the summer of 1955 when he approached a white woman working behind the counter of a grocery store. The details concerning what occurred next are at best sketchy. Conventional wisdom holds that he merely whistled at her. The writer William Bradford Huie, in a *Look* magazine expose, suggested that there was more of a sexual advance, that Till actually "squeezed her hand and said: 'How about a date, Baby?' … perhaps caught her at the waist, and said: 'You needn't be afraid o' me, Baby. I been with white girls before.'"[13] It is unlikely that the details of the subsequent tragedy will ever be completely ascertained. Such is the nature of the elusiveness involved in attempting to recreate the chain of events surrounding an encounter like what occurred between Till and the woman who caught his attention. But suffice it to say, the punishment Till received was in no way commensurate with what he said or did in the store.

Later that night, the woman's husband and his half brother drove to the home of Till's uncle, dragged the boy off, mutilated him beyond recognition, tied a cotton-gin fan around his neck, and tossed him into the Tallahatchie River. Campbell's first novel, *Your Blues Ain't Like Mine*, is largely a signification on this event in history. Armstrong Todd, born and raised in Chicago, has a "condescending" attitude toward the less sophisticated blacks who live in and around Hopewell, Mississippi. He contemplates how he will "*be glad to say goodbye to all these country fools.*" He is "city slick and so cool" that even in the white-owned pool hall, he is prone to use words such as "white-trash" and "crackers" in his boisterous diatribes. And then one day a white woman, Lily Cox, walks into the pool hall just as Todd is using French phrases that he learned from his father who had served in France during World War II. Todd is speaking to no one in particular, but just showing off as is his propensity. Though her husband, who owns the pool hall, had told her never to enter, Cox is fascinated by the black boy's facility with a foreign language and so the precarious chain of events proceeds from there.

She was standing at the door, peeking inside the poolroom with the exhilarated, frightened look of a girl sneaking her first drink behind a barn. The woman stepped inside, smiling at him as he spoke his

French phrases, and then she raised her hand and smelled her wrist and started laughing. Armstrong laughed too. The look in her eyes said that she'd done it, had the drink and not gotten caught.[14]

From that depiction, it seems that Cox is the one who initiates, however veiled, the forbidden social contact. Yet it is Todd who will pay the ultimate price as Cox's husband, in an act of so-called retribution, will shoot him point-blank with "no mercy."

History is full of examples similar to what occurred with Emmett Till and Campbell's fictional Armstrong Todd. And even in situations where these sorts of interracial encounters evolved into mutually consensual sexual relationships, black men have typically not fared very well as they often found themselves torn from the arms of their white beloved and (if they were able to escape a lynching) whisked off to answer in a court of law. Such was how it happened in the case of Jess Hollins in 1930s Oklahoma. The white woman he was with had voluntarily consorted with him, and she only "cried rape" when her brother-in-law stumbled upon the two of them together. Still, Hollins was tried and sentenced to death.

That same decade, in Alabama, Roosevelt Collins was executed for raping a white woman even though, off the record, the judge believed that Collins told the truth when he claimed that their relationship had been consensual. Evidently that judge believed also, as did the white jurors, that Collins, however innocent, still deserved the death sentence for "messin' around" with a white woman. In the Mississippi case of Willie McGee, it took the all-white jury a mere two and a half minutes to find him guilty of rape even though everyone in the black community knew that the relationship was consensual. However, fearing for their lives, those local blacks could not speak out and the whites, for their part, refused to acknowledge that a white woman would voluntarily have sex with a black man. And the notorious list goes on and on. The Giles brothers in Maryland in 1961. The Tarboro Three in North Carolina in 1973. All convicted and sentenced to death for raping white women when in actuality the relationships were consensual with no objection by the women until they were caught in the act by white men, whereupon the claim of "rape" was made in exchange, so to speak, for the white woman's exoneration.

The details read like a nightmare from the annals of slavery, until we look closely at the even more recent strange occurrences ranging from random car stops (white policemen pulling over black men who have a white woman passenger) to jailhouse suicides; from false arrests and the war against drugs (which some observers call the war against black men) to the loss of jobs due to "inappropriate" behavior. That last device is also used on occasion to keep white women in check although McClenney argues that it is the black man who suffers most in the fall-out from an interracial relationship. "She can always run to the white man," McClenney argues, "and he'll cover her ass and kick yours."[15] Even as he considers that danger, Campbell's Boone regards the white prize, Mallory Post, as being well worth the risk.

It is Hernton's belief that the sordid past involving interracial rela-tionships has made it so that — particularly in the case of black men and white women — contemporary such relationships cannot help but occur on a certain level of perversity. For the black man, the white woman becomes a thing that he acquires only at great risk to his life. And even when he does not seek her out, she looms as an ever-present threat to his security. Richard Wright was concerned about that reality as, in both "Big Boy Leaves Home" and *Native Son*, he has a young black man faced with his own eminent doom for the simple reason that a white woman is in the vicinity. And while the resulting atrocities have decreased in recent decades, sanctions that are more subtle remain in effect. Considering all this, one would think it is well nigh impossible for the black man and white woman to regard each other in terms of being just a man and a woman free from the psychological consequences of America's sad racial history.

Though, generally speaking, white women must publicly deny hav-ing any attraction to black men, there does exist what Hernton calls an "honest curiosity, or infatuation" that while usually curbed, does some-times evolve into intimacy. Psychiatrists William H. Grier and Price M. Cobbs echo Hernton's assessment that many such women are drawn to black men in response to what they perceive as the "exotic." Those psy-chiatrists contend that "the white woman who seeks a black lover finds him ... sufficiently strange, and she is able to experience the excitement of having a forbidden sexual object as well as a lover who is so different-looking as to allow her to see him as a different kind of human being."[16] I do not mean to suggest here that simple true love is never the moti-vating force behind two individuals of different races getting together. What I do mean to suggest though is that there are those who hide behind the ideal of "true love" so as to conceal a sexual yearning so humiliating in fact that few people want to discuss it.

Mallory Post's situation is especially complex because not only has she become the object of attention of her black male boss, but she is also having an affair with a married man who is ruthlessly capable of shifting from extreme possessiveness to utter neglect depending on how things are going for him with his wife at home. Having been an emotionally abused child, Post remains haunted by the memories of the times when her own father neglected her due to his belief that sons are more important than daughters. Moreover, she is trying to strike up a friendship with Esther Jackson though for a long time she cannot tell this black woman what has transpired between her and Boone since Jackson herself has a crush on the newly arrived black vice president. In her anthology essay, Campbell attempts to reconcile herself with the fact that black men and white women are dating each other with an ever increasing frequency. The author concedes, "My being angry isn't going to make white women and black men stop choosing each other."[17] But she also admits that she will always be uncomfortable at the sight of "black men with white women." It is the latter sentiment that Post recognizes as she tries to make progress in the relationship with her coworker Jackson.

Post never actually falls in love with Boone; in fact her feelings for him are ambiguous. Hernton argues that "some white women suffering from (among other things) racial guilt offer themselves to black men as a living symbol of atonement for the entire system of race prejudice in America."[18] Campbell tells us that Boone is astute enough concerning this phenomenon that "he knew a vulnerable white woman when he saw one." After scolding Post about prior racist practices of Angel City National Bank,

> he watched [her] face turn crimson and recognized it as the first blush of guilt. It was so easy to make certain white women feel guilty. He had learned in college that there were some white girls who wanted to atone for the sins of their forefathers, who would respond to his ranting and raving about the white man's injustice with rosy cheeks and sympathy…. white girls were prone to offer their bodies as consolation prizes. He had a sixth sense about such women.[19]

Boone considers himself adept at negotiating such relationships, but he perhaps is not so adept as, for example, *Brewster Place*'s Etta Johnson and Moreland Woods who were masters of the game in which they agreed to participate. Johnson, in that instance, wanted security and prestige; Woods just wanted her body. In that instance, the characters are of the same race which simplifies the matter somewhat. But Boone overestimates, in his relationship with Post, his own ability to fathom all the dynamics involved.

In his catalogue of things that white women like, Boone lists that "white girls liked the way brothers called them baby; it was something they couldn't get at home."[20] Perhaps there had been some white woman somewhere who became enamored by his use of that appellation, but it holds no special meaning for Post. On one occasion, she tells him, "You're a great looking guy and I really enjoyed being with you. If the circumstances were different...."[21] She does not finish her statement, but as she subsequently smiles, Boone imagines that "she was still playing her hard-to-get game." But the vice president is wrong once again since what she really wants to do is retreat alone into some private place where she can sort out her various emotions.

She primarily dates Boone because he is persistent and she does not want him to "think that she [is] a racist." But as it turns out, she actually enjoys kissing him and might even have allowed herself to "fall in love" but for the haunting vision of her father "watching, ... his huge face contorted with anger." She conforms to the sexual taboo that prohibits her from having a relationship with Boone and in the aftermath wants to "talk everything over with Esther. But the black woman might ask her questions she didn't want to answer."[22]

Post also rejects intimacy with Boone because, as I mentioned earlier, she is already involved with someone else, though that someone else happens to be a married man. Yet when he stands her up for the umpteenth time, she plots her revenge and uses Boone to put her plan into effect. Having earlier resisted dating Boone anymore, she now changes her mind and invites him to the Beverly Hills Society's annual dinner, which she knows her married boyfriend will be attending with his wife. This jilted younger woman then parades her black date in front of her boyfriend and even goes so far as to introduce the two men whereupon Boone "read in the white man's eyes ... an unmistakable desire to inflict pain — possibly genital mutilation."[23] Post thus has succeeded in making her white lover not just jealous but murderously enraged.

Three decades before *Brothers and Sisters*, Hernton had already noted how "some white women 'play up' to black men in public or at parties as a kind of *threat* to extract favor or attention from, or to arouse jealousy in, their own men."[24] Hernton further offered the example of a married white woman who made it a point to flaunt herself in front of a black graduate student right in the presence of her husband. According to the student, she insisted on dancing with him "very close up" and in the car "she started bumping into me, rubbing her legs against mine, and bouncing her breasts around in my face."[25] When the woman and her husband got home, he beat her but then "made love to her like he never had before," all in an effort to compete against the black man in whom his wife had expressed an interest.

Post's married lover similarly responds in dramatic fashion. At 6:00 A.M. in the morning after the Beverly Hills dinner, he calls her and demands to know, "Are you fucking that nigger?" She hangs up the phone and he immediately calls again wanting to know the same thing. She hangs up again and this time she cuts on the answering machine, and all he can do is issue one apology after another, begging to speak to her, promising to divorce his wife as soon as he can. Before the day is over, he has sent enough roses for Post to decorate every room in her town house. All because she dated a black man.

But there is always an element of danger. The woman in Hernton's example is physically beaten. Post's married lover is at a point where it seems he could castrate Boone. Kirk Madison, the interim vice president before Boone's arrival, even gets angry when he sees Boone and Post simply talking for a while after departmental meetings have been adjourned.

> He wants her. The thought detonated in Kirk's mind.... He fought the urge, a powerful one, to leap on Humphrey and punch him until he saw blood spurting from every opening in his face. He could feel his own fist against the black man's jaw.... He should smile at his own women.[26]

Madison's feeling that Boone should smile only "at his own women" reminds us of Hernton's assertion that "when a black man is intimate with *one* white woman, in the minds and emotions of the white man, that black man is intimate with *all* white women."[27] One tends to want to quarrel with how Hernton generalizes about the issue since not all white men view the black man with a white woman as an intimacy involving every white woman. Yet many white men do as they register their opposition to miscegenation, claiming it as a threat to white racial purity.

That alleged fear becomes rather absurd as one thinks back to the miscegenation that persisted during slavery, only then it was white men who forced their intentions on helpless slave women. Obviously, miscegenation has been part of the American panorama since this country's beginnings. Many white men prefer not to see black men with white women due to a sense that now the tables are turned. Instead of the white man having unbridled access to the black woman, it is now the black man who engages in intimacy with the white woman, sometimes (as Hernton and Campbell attest) strictly for revenge.

Hernton gives the example of a black man at a party who whisks a white woman away from her white male companion and then goes through a ritual of grabbing her buttocks, fondling her breasts, and kissing her, all right there on the dance floor. The black man wants to make her escort mad, and he constantly peers at him to ascertain whether his actions have been successful. Indeed the white escort becomes furious, and the black man revels in his success much like Boone at the Beverly Hills dinner, perceiving himself as a conqueror of sorts thinking "Yeah, white boy. Your woman is with me."

I must reiterate here that I certainly mean to cast no blanket aspersions at those who have been involved in interracial relationships. But there is fault to be found in a person like Boone who thinks that if he was to enter into a relationship with a black woman, it would be "just two black people, and there was no status in that. A sister was just a sister, too devalued on the common market to really matter."[28] In her essay "If the Present Looks Like the Past, What Does the Future Look Like?," Alice Walker says that "a look at the photographs of the women chosen by our male leaders is, in many ways, chilling."[29] Walker supplies us with an extensive list of black men who have been important race leaders but who nevertheless chose wives based on, as Walker puts it, the "nearness of their complexions to white." It is the same phenomenon that Jackson witnesses in her brother, the lawyer, whose wife's "skin was so fair that several glances were required to verify that she was black.... In the eight years that her brother had been married, she had not forgiven him for choosing someone with hair that blew in the wind.... It was a betrayal that continued to wound."[30] And here is where I think Hernton misses the boat, so to speak, in his characterization of the black woman as misguided in her response to the dwindling population of black men from which she might choose a mate. Citing one black woman in particular who accuses black men of "betraying the race," Hernton asserts that such a response "does not reflect much analytical objectivity." In a sense Hernton is right. Many black women do not assess the situation with absolute objectivity. Indeed they have become increasingly passionate about what the consequences will be for them with regard to the social dilemma. But these black women are not as far from the mark as Hernton would have us believe.

According to him, black women who are alarmed about black man/white woman relationships "are reacting out of the same race-sex-jealousy emotional syndrome as is a white man who is alarmed over white women and black men."[31] But that comparison is inappropriate. While some white men might feel sexually inadequate in the presence of a black man who is with a white woman, it does not compare to what bell hooks refers to as a certain anxiety that "is intensified for black women, because we suffer under the tyranny of a white aesthetic that teaches us how to appear in order to be seen as beautiful, even as it simultaneously teaches us that we can never make it."[32] So often, even now, if a white man is jealous he can apply sanctions of the sort that McClenney has in mind when he warns that "the white man will use his women to set you up." Indeed this is what happens in *Your Blues Ain't Like Mine* when Lily Cox is forced, during the sheriff's questioning, to "think of something to say ... that wouldn't make Floyd angry." When the sheriff asks whether or not Todd was "bothering" her, she has only to answer "I'm ashamed to say what he done," and the wrath of southern law comes crashing down on Todd's head. Cox is even able to reconcile herself with the tragedy by convincing herself that "there was no telling what that freckle-faced boy might have done if Floyd hadn't come along and saved her."[33]

That was 1955, but forty years later, as we see in Campbell's second novel, the dangers have hardly subsided at all. Having used Boone to make her boyfriend jealous, Post has no further need for him and seeks now to break off their social relationship. Desperately trying to change her mind, that vice president accidentally tears her blouse and so is destined to a fate that is only a modern version of what happened once Bigger Thomas (in Richard Wright's *Native Son*) found himself in the bedroom of a young white woman. Writing in 1993, Arnold Rampersad explains the significance of race and sexuality as Wright had explored it in *Native Son* and as it continues to be a cornerstone of race relations today. Says Rampersad,

> Wright ... understood fully ... that there could be no truly probing discussion of the subject of race in America without extended reference to questions of sexuality and miscegenation. After his arrest,

Bigger Thomas is falsely accused of the rape of Mary Dalton.... Because the sexuality of white women is flaunted in movies and magazines but absolutely forbidden to black men, Bigger and men like him sometimes develop a potentially murderous fixation on these women. Rape may then acquire the illusion of being a political act; but the underlying threat to women is real and deadly.[34]

Rampersad reiterates what both Hernton and Campbell understood to be the consequences of the American racial dilemma as pertains to the individuals most vulnerable. How do the broad range of black men, from Bigger Thomas to Humphrey Boone, manage in a world where the female ideal is almost always white? What does it mean to be a white woman propped up on the eternal pedestal?

It had not occurred to Post to accuse Boone of attempted rape until Bailey Reynolds, the president's white assistant, planted the seeds in her mind: "He ripped your blouse. He grabbed you....you don't know what might have happened if someone hadn't come in."[35] So what had actually been an accident turns into attempted rape since Post, like Cox, is in no position to contest Reynolds' insistence on racial solidarity in this the most crucial of matters. As Cox and many other white women have had to do when confronted by white male authority, Post has to go along with "the program" even though Boone will be forced to resign from his job. We had seen the same strategy for the black man's removal in Wade's *Company Man*. Of all Covington's "transgressions," it is the so-called "impropriety" with a white secretary that finally sealed his doom. Unable to get an erection, he had nevertheless "kissed her with a drunk's sloppy precision" and wound up "in [her] hotel room, lying on her bed, waiting for her to emerge from the bathroom, in all likelihood naked from tit to toe."[36] As contrived as his boss's later assessment will be, Covington is nonetheless left unemployed with the charge of sexual harassment hanging forever over his head.

That black executive cannot escape the thought that his grandmother, though dead, is still somewhere chastising him, apprising him that *"you just another nigga now."* Likewise, Boone recalls how, in the midst of his meteoric rise to prominence, his sister had warned him, "One of these days, you gone remember exactly what it's like to be a nigger."[37] As *Brothers and Sisters* concludes, we are further made to consider what Boone's coworker Jackson had surmised in declaring that "any black person in America who isn't bitter is either dead or psychotic."[38]

We certainly have the evidence (in the literature discussed in this study as well as in the real world) for each of her three tragic stipulations — bitterness, death, and insanity. But even more frightening is the lingering prospect that behind someone's mask of emotional stability lies the soul of a person on the verge of exploding with no hint of the psychological devastation that was smoldering there all along.

Conclusion

Brothers and Sisters ends on a high note with the Solid Rock Baptist Church sponsoring an African family reunion which suggests, for the reader, a future wherein black achievement and self-appreciation will finally be realized. The Reverend Odell Rice had been pushing the notion that more blacks should go into business so as not to have to depend on white enterprise. By the end of the novel, a Solid Rock National Bank has been chartered and Boone is all set to become the bank's chief executive officer.

Yet we should recall how at an earlier stage in Campbell's career, she was inclined to dispose of difficult issues with the greatest amount of optimism that she could muster. So it is particularly useful to consider how Wade's Bill Covington, at the point of becoming a parent, is not joyous at all but instead prone to grieve because "all that baby has to look forward to is more of the same. The same eventual alienation, the same de facto isolation, the same inescapable sentence of unbelonging, of being thingafied."[1] By having his main character thus contemplate, Wade causes us to wonder what the likelihood is that relations between the races will be all that different in the future. What conditions will tomorrow's children have to accede to in order to be socially accepted?

Ex-Coloured Man's narrator offers the proposition that, for those light-complected enough to do it, "passing" is a viable solution. I would take it even further and offer the prospect that while not literally passing, many blacks do undergo a psychological transition into the realm of whiteness, under the presumption that their lives will be greatly enhanced. It is the compromise that O.J. Simpson entered into as he undertook the challenge of elocution classes on the road to becoming a corporate spokesman. He was, as *Newsweek*'s Ellis Cose asserts, "supposed to have transcended race," supposed to have made it to the point where he could with confidence say that his "biggest accomplishment was getting people to look at me like a man first, not a black man."[2] A theoretically laudable goal perhaps, until it becomes clearer exactly what is being traded away.

Johnson's narrator was light enough to pass while those who were darker had to settle — when such a path seemed appropriate to them — for the mental conversion to whiteness. The latter of course was the choice of Simpson. But now in this age of medical breakthroughs, even darker-skinned blacks have the means at their disposal to effect what Michael Awkward has termed "transraciality." In *Negotiating Difference*, that critic offers the following distinction:

> Passing requires that its participants be born with physical charac-
> teristics associated with the racial other. By contrast, transraciality
> as a mode of masquerade necessitates the radical revision of one's
> natural markings and the adoption of aspects of the human surface
> (especially skin, hair, and facial features) generally associated with
> the racial other…. But while passing serves as a form through which
> we can interrogate some of the implications of America's one-drop
> rule of racial designation … transraciality … offers an even more
> effective means of uncovering the constructedness of the rules of
> racial being. …Transraciality represents an individually determined,
> surgically — and/or cosmetically — assisted traversal of boundaries.[3]

I would argue that passing as a social phenomenon had already uncov-
ered as profoundly as anything the "constructedness of the rules of racial being." And the act of denying one's race in a final self-negating way (which I take "passing" to be) is just as startling a commentary as the process whereby a person has one operation after another, striving for a whiteness that will never be fully attained.

Those strategies in themselves speak volumes to the status of blacks in America. Our social condition is one from which we, more often than not, have had to construct some means of escape or means of adapta-
tion. Over the years, some of us opted to pass; others, especially in more recent times, have embarked on the path of cosmetic surgery. What could be more extreme than those two measures? The answer, I would argue, points to an even greater tragedy, that is the manner in which we have altered the state of our inner being in one final act of adjustment.

Notes

Preface

1. John Jay Osborn, *The Paper Chase* (1971; New York: Avon, 1973) 18–19.

2. Scott Turow, *One L* (1977; New York: Penguin, 1983) 118–19.

3. Bebe Moore Campbell, *Brothers and Sisters* (New York: Putnam, 1994) 141.

4. Gloria Naylor, *Bailey's Cafe* (1992; New York: Vintage, 1993) 207.

5. Gloria Naylor, *Linden Hills* (1985; New York: Penguin, 1986) 106.

6. Margaret Homans, "The Woman in the Cave: Recent Feminist Fictions and the Classical World," *Contemporary Literature* 29 (1988): 387.

7. Ishmael Reed, *Japanese by Spring* (New York: Atheneum, 1993) 12–13.

Young Mr. Emerson's Crucial Message

1. Ralph Ellison, *Invisible Man* (1952; New York: Vintage, 1972) 183.

2. Ellison, *Invisible Man* 184.

3. J.D. Salinger, *The Catcher in the Rye* (1951; New York: Bantam, 1981) 192.

4. Ellison, *Invisible Man* 190.

5. Ellison, *Invisible Man* 171.

6. Ellison, *Invisible Man* 54.

7. Ellison, *Invisible Man* 136.

8. Ellison, *Invisible Man* 136.

9. Ellison, *Invisible Man* 139

10. Ellison, *Invisible Man* 139.

11. Ellison, *Invisible Man* 147.

12. Ralph Waldo Emerson, "Self-Reliance," *Ralph Waldo Emerson*, ed. Richard Poirer (New York: Oxford University Press, 1990) 132–33.

13. Ralph Ellison, "Hidden Name and Complex Fate," *Shadow and Act* (1964; New York: Vintage, 1972) 153.

14. James Alan McPherson, "Indivisible Man," *The Atlantic Monthly* Dec. 1970: 46.

15. Ellison, *Invisible Man* 10.

16. Ralph Ellison, "The Little Man at Chehaw Station," *Going to the Territory* (New York: Random, 1986) 16.

17. Ellison, *Invisible Man* 568.

18. Sharon Begley, "Three Is Not Enough: Surprising New Lessons from the Controversial Science of Race," *Newsweek* Feb. 13, 1995: 67.

19. Houston A. Baker, "A Forgotten Prototype: *The Autobiography of an Ex-Colored Man* and *Invisible Man*," *The Virginia Quarterly Review* 49 (1973).

20. James Weldon Johnson, *The Autobiography of an Ex-Coloured Man* (1912; New York: Hill and Wang, 1981) 21.

21. Emerson, "Experience," *Ralph Waldo Emerson* 226.

22. Emerson, "Experience" 217.

23. Ellison, *Invisible Man* 186.

24. Ellison, *Invisible Man* 179.

25. Walt Whitman, "Earth, My Likeness," *Complete Poetry and Selected Prose*, ed. James E. Miller (Boston: Houghton Mifflin, 1959) 96.

26. Whitman, "What Think You I Take My Pen in Hand?", *Complete Poetry and Selected Prose* 97.

27. Jo Ann Lee, "Special Problems of Older Gay Employees," *Homosexual Issues in the Workplace*, ed. Louis Diamant (Washington, D.C.: Taylor and Francis, 1993) 219–20.

28. Laura Blumenfeld, "The Ghost of *Philadelphia*: A Real-Life AIDS-Discrimination Case Returns to Haunt a Senate Candidate," *The Washington Post* 25 Jan. 1994: C4.

29. Whitman, "To a Stranger," *Complete Poetry and Selected Prose* 93.

30. Ellison, *Invisible Man* 182.

31. Emerson, "The American Scholar," *Ralph Waldo Emerson* 52.

32. Ellison, "What America Would Be Like Without Blacks," *Going to the Territory* 110–11.

33. Ellison, *Invisible Man* 204.

34. Ellison, *Invisible Man* 16.

35. Joel Chandler Harris, "How Mr. Rabbit Was Too Sharp for Mr. Fox," *Uncle Remus: His Songs and His Sayings* (New York: D. Appleton, 1881) 30–31.

36. Ellison, "Hidden Name and Complex Fate," *Shadow and Act* 147.

37. Booker T. Washington, *Up From Slavery* (1901; New York: Bantam, 1970) 165.

38. Ellison, *Invisible Man* 100.

39. Paul Laurence Dunbar, "We Wear the Mask," *The Complete Poems of Paul Laurence Dunbar* (New York: Dodd, 1948) 112–13.

40. Ellison, *Invisible Man* 116–17.

41. Ellison, *Invisible Man* 36.

42. W. E. B. Du Bois, *The Souls of Black Folk* (1903; Greenwich, Connecticut: Fawcett, 1961) 48.

43. Washington, *Up from Slavery* 156.

44. Emma Thornbrough, "Booker T. Washington as Seen by His White Contemporaries," *The Journal of Negro History* 53 (1968): 162.

45. Ellison, *Invisible Man* 142.

46. Ellison, *Invisible Man* 183.

47. Leonard Deutsch, "Ralph Waldo Ellison and Ralph Waldo Emerson: A Shared Moral Vision," *CLA Journal* 16 (1972): 165.

48. Ellison, *Invisible Man* 92.

49. Calvin Hernton, *Sex and Racism in America* (1965; New York: Anchor, 1992) 52–53.

"What Shall a Man Give in Exchange for His Soul?"

1. Gloria Naylor, *Linden Hills* (1985; New York: Penguin, 1986) 104.

2. Naylor, *Linden Hills* 110.

3. Naylor, *Linden Hills* 100.

4. Bebe Moore Campbell, "Black Executives and Corporate Stress," *The New York Times Magazine* Dec. 12, 1982: 39.

5. George Davis and Glegg Watson, *Black Life in Corporate America: Swimming in the Mainstream* (New York: Anchor, 1982) 38.

6. Naylor, *Linden Hills* 104.

7. Naylor, *Linden Hills* 53.

8. Naylor, *Linden Hills* 109.

9. Naylor, *Linden Hills* 106.

10. Naylor, *Linden Hills* 102.

11. Naylor, *Linden Hills* 77.

12. Margaret Homans, "The Woman in the Cave: Recent Fictions and the Classical Underworld," *Contemporary Literature* 29 (1988): 378.

13. Naylor, *Linden Hills* 78.

14. Naylor, *Linden Hills* 224.

15. Naylor, *Linden Hills* 226–27.

16. Naylor, *Linden Hills* 231.

17. E. Franklin Frazier, *Black Bourgeoisie* (1957; New York: Free Press, 1965) 24.

18. Naylor, *Linden Hills* 236.

19. Naylor, *Linden Hills* 244.

20. Naylor, *Linden Hills* 182.

21. Barbara Christian, "Gloria Naylor's Geography: Community, Class, and Patriarchy in *The Women of Brewster Place* and *Linden Hills*," *Reading Black, Reading Feminist*, ed. Henry Louis Gates (New York: Meridian, 1990) 367.

22. Gloria Naylor, *The Women of Brewster Place* (1982; New York: Penguin, 1983) 86.

23. Naylor, *Brewster Place* 87.

24. Naylor, *Brewster Place* 88.

25. Arthur Miller, *Death of a Salesman* (1949; New York: Viking, 1971) 23.

26. Naylor, *Linden Hills* 236.

27. Naylor, *Brewster Place* 81.

28. Ellis Cose, *The Rage of a Privileged Class* (New York: Harper-Collins, 1993) 89.

29. Reginald Lewis and Blair Walker, *"Why Should White Guys Have All the Fun?": How Reginald Lewis Created a Billion-Dollar Business Empire* (New York: John Wiley, 1995) 75.

30. Cose, *Rage* 89.

31. Peter Annin, "The Corporation: Allstate Saw the Light When It Started Following the Money," *Newsweek* Apr. 3, 1995: 32.

32. Naylor, *Linden Hills* 106.

33. Homans, "Woman in the Cave" 387.

34. Gloria Naylor, *Bailey's Cafe* (1992; New York: Vintage, 1993) 196.

35. Naylor, *Bailey's Cafe* 197.

36. August Meier and Elliott Rudwick, *Black Detroit and the Rise of the UAW* (1979; New York: Oxford University Press, 1981) 7–8.

37. Naylor, *Bailey's Cafe* 173.

38. Naylor, *Bailey's Cafe* 179.

39. Naylor, *Bailey's Cafe* 186.

40. Naylor, *Bailey's Cafe* 180.

41. Naylor, *Bailey's Cafe* 186.

42. John T. Molloy, *Dress for Success* (New York: Peter Wyden, 1975) 152.

43. Earl McClenney, *How to Survive When You're the Only Black in the Office* (Richmond, Virginia: First Associates, 1987) 196.

44. Malcolm X, "Message to the Grass Roots," *Malcolm X Speaks*, ed. George Breitman (1965; New York: Grove, 1966) 10–11.

45. Jonathan Kaufman, "Black Executives Say Prejudice Still Impedes Their Path to the Top," *The Wall Street Journal* 9 July 1980: 1.

46. Lawrence Otis Graham, *Member of the Club* (New York: Harper-Collins, 1995) 71.

47. Kaufman, "Black Executives" 1.

48. Naylor, *Bailey's Cafe* 212.

49. Campbell, "Black Executives" 39.

50. McClenney, *How to Survive* 140.

51. Ellison, *Invisible Man* 260.

52. Johnson, *Ex-Coloured* 211.

53. Naylor, *Bailey's Cafe* 212.

54. Joleen Kirschenman and Kathryn Neckerman, "'We'd Love to Hire Them, But ...': The Meaning of Race for Employers," *The Urban Underclass,* ed. Christopher Jencks and Paul Peterson (Washington, D.C.: Brookings Institution, 1991) 208.

"Torn Asunder"

1. Du Bois, *Souls of Black Folk* 16–17.

2. Naylor, *Bailey's Cafe* 211.

3. Brent Wade, *Company Man* (1992; New York: Anchor, 1993) 9.

4. Salinger, *Catcher* 191–92.

5. Joseph Heller, *Something Happened* (New York: Knopf, 1974) 417.

6. Wade 13.

7. Wade 14.

8. Wade 14.

9. Bebe Moore Campbell, "Blacks Who Live in a White World," *Ebony* March 1982: 142.

10. Kathy Russell, Midge Wilson, and Ronald Hall, *The Color Complex: The Politics of Skin Color Among African Americans* (1992; New York: Anchor, 1993) 27.

11. Wade 14.

12. "White Male Executives Haven't Changed Ways," *Jet* 21 June 1993: 28.

13. Wade 49.

14. Wade 18.

15. Zora Neale Hurston, *Their Eyes Were Watching God* (1937; New York: Perennial, 1990) 40–41.

16. Hurston 33.

17. Wade 48.

18. Wade 49.

19. Wade 50.

20. Wade 16.

21. Wade 17.

22. David Wilkins, "Two Paths to the Mountaintop?: The Role of Legal Education in Shaping the Values of Black Corporate Lawyers," *Stanford Law Review* 45 (1993): 1990.

23. Wade 177.

24. Malcolm X, "Message to the Grass Roots" 16–17.

25. Wade 178.

26. Wade 50.

27. Wade 37.

28. Wade 12.

29. Ossie Davis, "On Malcolm X" (afterword), *The Autobiography of Malcolm X*, by Malcolm X and Alex Haley (New York: Grove, 1966) 458.

30. Heller 368.

31. Davis 457.

32. Wade 66.

33. Wade 205.

34. Wade 205.

35. Wade 205.

36. Davis 458.

37. Wade 217.

38. Heller 561.

39. Wade 217.

Black Studies and the Academy

1. Wade 57.

2. Reed, *Japanese by Spring* 11.

3. Reed, *Japanese by Spring* 11.

4. Reed, *Japanese by Spring* 17.

5. Jon Ewing, "The Great Tenure Battle of 1977" (interview with Ishmael Reed), *Shrovetide in Old New Orleans*, ed. Ishmael Reed (Garden City, New York: Doubleday, 1978) 226.

6. McClenney, *How to Survive* 140.

7. Jay Parini, "Tenure and the Loss of Faculty Talent," *The Chronicle of Higher Education* 14 July 1995: A40.

8. Reed, *Japanese by Spring* 10.

9. Mel Watkins, "An Interview with Ishmael Reed," *The Southern Review* 21 (1985): 605.

10. Ishmael Reed, "Hoodoo Manifesto #2 on Criticism: The Baker-Gayle Fallacy," *Umum Newsletter* 4. 3–4 (1975): 9.

11. Henry Louis Gates, *Figures in Black* (New York: Oxford University Press, 1989) 57.

12. Houston Baker, "Generational Shifts and Afro-American Literature," *The Critical Tradition,* ed. David Richter (New York: St. Martin's, 1989) 1367.

13. Sandra Adell, *Double-Consciousness/Double Bind* (Urbana: University of Illinois Press, 1994) 137.

14. Reed, *Japanese by Spring* 31.

15. Reed, "Hoodoo Manifesto" 8.

16. Ishmael Reed, *The Free-Lance Pallbearers* (1967; Chatham, New Jersey: Chatham, 1975) 20.

17. Reed, *Japanese by Spring* 32.

18. Reed, "Hoodoo Manifesto" 11.

19. Fenton Bailey, *Fall from Grace: The Untold Story of Michael Milken* (New York: Birch Lane, 1992) 202.

20. Reed, *Japanese by Spring* 85.

21. John Byrne and Chuck Hawkins, "Executive Pay: The Party Ain't Over Yet," *Business Week* 26 April 1993: 57.

22. Reed, *Japanese by Spring* 40.

23. Reed, *Japanese by Spring* 41.

24. Jack London, "The Yellow Peril," *Revolution and Other Essays* (New York: MacMillan, 1910) 285.

25. Jack London, "The Unparalleled Invasion," *The Strength of the Strong* (New York: MacMillan, 1914) 100.

26. Lawrence Biemiller, "Vitriolic Student Paper Is Causing Lasting Harm, Many at Dartmouth Say," *The Chronicle of Higher Education* 8 Feb. 1989: A15.

27. Biemiller A14.

28. Audre Lorde, "The Master's Tools Will Never Dismantle the Master's House," *Sister Outsider: Essays and Speeches* (Trumansburg, New York: Crossing Press, 1984) 110.

29. Henry Louis Gates, "'What's Love Got to Do with It?': Critical Theory, Integrity, and the Black Idiom," *New Literary History* 18 (1987): 357.

30. Joyce A. Joyce, "'Who the Cap Fit': Unconsciousness and Unconscionableness in the Criticism of Houston A. Baker, Jr., and Henry Louis Gates, Jr.," *New Literary History* 18 (1987): 377.

31. Reed, *Japanese by Spring* 43.

32. Reed, *Japanese by Spring* 47.

33. Marcia Westkott, "Women's Studies as a Strategy for Change: Between Criticism and Vision," *Theories of Women's Studies,* ed. Gloria Bowles and Renate Duelli Klein (Boston: Routledge, 1983) 212.

34. Heller, *Something Happened* 13.

35. Courtney Leatherman, "Abolition of Tenure Rattles Faculty at College of Ozarks," *The Chronicle of Higher Education* 26 Jan. 1994: A18.

From Freelance Writer to Corporate Token

1. Patrice Gaines, *Laughing in the Dark* (New York: Crown, 1994) 241.

2. Jill Nelson, *Volunteer Slavery* (Chicago: Noble, 1993) 137.

3. Matilda Butler, William Paisley, Suzanne Pingree, and Robert Hawkins, *Women and the Mass Media* (New York: Human Sciences, 1980) 227.

4. Julia Lawlor, "Executive Exodus," *Working Woman* Nov. 1994: 40.

5. United States Department of Labor, Women's Bureau, *Working Women Count!* (Washington, D.C.: Department of Labor, 1994) 4.

6. Nelson 67.

7. Nelson 53.

8. Nelson 53.

9. Nelson 10.

10. Harriet Jacobs, *Incidents in the Life of a Slave Girl* (1861; Cambridge: Harvard University Press, 1987) 35.

11. Nelson 15.

12. Russell, et. al., *Color Complex* 38.

13. Russell 39.

14. Nelson 56.

15. Nelson 57.

16. Nelson 72-73.

17. Nelson 74.

18. Ralph Gomes and Linda Faye Williams, "Race and Crime: The Role of the Media in Perpetuating Racism and Classism in America," *Sources: Notable Selections in Race and Ethnicity*, ed. Adalberto Aguirre and David Baker (Guilford, Connecticut: Dushkin, 1995) 344.

19. Nelson 72.

20. Nathan McCall, *Makes Me Wanna Holler: A Young Black Man in America* (New York: Random, 1994) 380–81.

21. Nelson 63.

22. Gaines 242.

23. Nelson 75.

24. Nelson 77.

25. Nelson 53.

26. Nelson 60.

27. Leith Mullings, "Images, Ideology, and Women of Color," *Women of Color in U.S. Society*, ed. Maxine Baca Zinn and Bonnie Thornton Dill (Philadelphia: Temple University Press, 1994) 282–83.

28. Jacobs 33.

29. bell hooks, *Ain't I a Woman* (1981; Boston: South End, 1992) 154.

30. Nelson 84–85.
31. Nelson 87.
32. Nelson 93.
33. Nelson 144.
34. McClenney, *How to Survive* 180.
35. Nelson 196–97.
36. Nelson 197.
37. Nelson 85.
38. Nelson 213.

Our Pathological Inheritance

1. Henry Louis Gates, *The Signifying Monkey: A Theory of Afro-American Literary Criticism* (New York: Oxford University Press, 1988) xxiv.
2. Gates, *Signifying Monkey* 120.
3. Gates, *Signifying Monkey* 124.
4. Bebe Moore Campbell, "Polishing Your Business Image," *Essence* Mar. 1984: 128.
5. Campbell, "Blacks Who Live in a White World" 141.
6. Bebe Moore Campbell, "Black Men, White Women: A Sister Relinquishes Her Anger," *Wild Women Don't Wear No Blues: Black Women Writers on Love, Men, and Sex*, ed. Marita Golden (New York: Doubleday, 1993) 117.
7. Richard Wright, *Lawd Today* (1963; New York: Avon, 1969) 27.
8. Wright 27–28.
9. Calvin Hernton, *Sex and Racism in America* (1965; New York: Anchor, 1992) 62–63.
10. Bebe Moore Campbell, *Brothers and Sisters* (New York: Putnam's, 1994) 319.
11. Hernton 74.
12. McClenney, *How to Survive* 15.
13. William Bradford Huie, "The Shocking Story of Approved Killing in Mississippi," *Look* 24 Jan. 1956: 46.
14. Bebe Moore Campbell, *Your Blues Ain't Like Mine* (1992; New York: Ballantine, 1993) 19.
15. McClenney 17.
16. William Grier and Price Cobbs, *Black Rage* (1968; New York: Basic, 1992) 93.
17. Campbell, "Black Men, White Women" 124.
18. Hernton 44.

19. Campbell, *Brothers and Sisters* 297.
20. Campbell, *Brothers and Sisters* 419.
21. Campbell, *Brothers and Sisters* 384.
22. Campbell, *Brothers and Sisters* 385.
23. Campbell, *Brothers and Sisters* 374.
24. Hernton 40.
25. Hernton 41.
26. Campbell, *Brothers and Sisters* 365.
27. Hernton 122.
28. Campbell, *Brothers and Sisters* 391.
29. Alice Walker, "If the Present Looks Like the Past, What Does the Future Look Like?," *In Search of Our Mothers' Gardens* (1982; San Diego: Harvest, 1983) 302.
30. Campbell, *Brothers and Sisters* 344–45.
31. Hernton 142.
32. bell hooks, "Appearance Obsession: Is the Price Too High?," *Essence* Aug. 1995: 70.
33. Campbell, *Your Blues* 47.
34. Arnold Rampersad, introduction, *Native Son*, by Richard Wright (1940; New York: HarperPerennial, 1993) xxii.
35. Campbell, *Brothers and Sisters* 434.
36. Wade, *Company Man* 198–99.
37. Campbell, *Brothers and Sisters* 448.
38. Campbell, *Brothers and Sisters* 440.

Conclusion

1. Wade, *Company Man* 132.
2. Ellis Cose, "Caught Between Two Worlds: Why Simpson Couldn't Overcome the Barriers of Race," *Newsweek* 11 July 1994: 28.
3. Michael Awkward, *Negotiating Difference: Race, Gender, and the Politics of Positionality* (Chicago: University of Chicago Press, 1995) 180.

Annotated Bibliography

Adell, Sandra. *Double-Consciousness/Double Bind*. Urbana: University of Illinois Press, 1994.
   Duality of consciousness can exist on a variety of levels. Adell begins by elaborating on how W.E.B. Du Bois was substantially influenced by Eurocentric philosophers. Black feminist literary discourse, even while establishing new ideologies, remains rooted in the systems of generations past. Finally, Adell argues that critics in general can find themselves in the rather paradoxical position of having to abandon certain theories that they themselves helped to create.

Annin, Peter. "The Corporation: Allstate Saw the Light When It Started Following the Money." *Newsweek* (Apr. 3, 1995): 32–33.
   During the period from the mid–1970s to the mid–1990s, Allstate Insurance undertook an extensive affirmative action plan. The plan was not one forced upon the company by government, but one that the company itself initiated in large part to capitalize on an untapped market of prospective black customers.

Awkward, Michael. *Negotiating Difference: Race, Gender, and the Politics of Positionality*. Chicago: University of Chicago Press, 1995.
   Looking at a wide variety of creative writers, literary critics, and popular culture personalities, Awkward evaluates the ways in which they adjusted themselves in order to bridge what might otherwise have been substantial gaps caused by racial and gender difference.

Bailey, Fenton. *Fall From Grace: The Untold Story of Michael Milken*. New York: Birch Lane, 1992.
   During the 1980s, Michael Milken manipulated the investment market by alternately inflating and deflating the value of junk bonds. He gained a reputation as the junk bond king with a salary so large that it made it into *The Guiness Book of Records*. Yet, his investment activities were illegal and he eventually was charged with criminal conduct stemming from Securities and Exchange violations.

Baker, Houston. "A Forgotten Prototype: *The Autobiography of an Ex-Colored Man* and *Invisible Man*." *The Virginia Quarterly Review* 49 (1973): 433–49.

Invisible Man is part of an extensive African American literary tradition that includes writers such as Britton Hammon, Frederick Douglass, Langston Hughes, and Richard Wright. However, similarities between Ellison's novel and Johnson's *The Autobiography of an Ex-Coloured Man* are especially profound.

_____. "Generational Shifts and Afro-American Literature." In *The Critical Tradition*, edited by David Richter, 1344–73. New York: St. Martin's, 1989.

Baker acknowledges the arrival of a new era of black literary criticism that has been shaped in large part by the emergence of theorist Henry Louis Gates. Nevertheless, says Baker, folklore and the sociological conditions that characterize black life should not be reduced in significance as new schools of literary thought come to the fore.

Begley, Sharon. "Three Is Not Enough: Surprising New Lessons from the Controversial Science of Race." *Newsweek* (Feb. 13, 1995): 67–69.

Efforts to classify people in accordance with what is actually a limited number of racial categories is, as it turns out, a seriously flawed endeavor.

Biemiller, Lawrence. "Vitriolic Student Paper Is Causing Lasting Harm, Many at Dartmouth Say." *The Chronicle of Higher Education* (Feb. 8, 1989): A1, A14-A15.

A conservative student-run newspaper, the *Dartmouth Review*, is the center of much debate on that college campus. The paper urges that more academic attention should be afforded Western civilization and less should be afforded to programs such as Afro-American, Native American, and Women's Studies.

Blumenfeld, Laura. "The Ghost of *Philadelphia*: A Real-Life AIDS-Discrimination Case Returns to Haunt a Senate Candidate." *The Washington Post* (Jan. 25, 1994): C1, C4.

Clarence Cain, a promising young lawyer, was fired from Hyatt Legal Services after it was discovered that he had contracted AIDS. Just before he died, he won a lawsuit against that corporation. Though the producers of the movie *Philadelphia* insist that they did not rely on any one legal case, the parallels between the movie and Cain's later life are undeniable.

Butler, Matilda, William Paisley, Suzanne Pingree, and Robert Hawkins. *Women and the Mass Media*. New York: Human Services, 1980.

Relying on data from scientific studies, these authors expose the inequities that exist between men and women in all areas of the media including newspapers, magazines, radio, and television.

Byrne, John, and Chuck Hawkins. "Executive Pay: The Party Ain't Over Yet." *Business Week* (Apr. 26, 1993): 56–57, 59–62, 64.
  A study of the skyrocketing salaries of corporate chief executive officers.

Campbell, Bebe Moore. "Black Executives and Corporate Stress." *The New York Times Magazine* (Dec. 12, 1982): 36–39, 100, 102, 104–7.
  Black managers in largely white companies are a relatively recent phenomenon. In negotiating their climbs up corporate ladders, these black executives often have to "straddle two worlds," one black and one white. Isolation and loneliness are often the result, and sometimes even loss of identity.

_____. "Black Men, White Women: A Sister Relinquishes Her Anger." In *Wild Women Don't Wear No Blues: Black Women Writers on Love, Men, and Sex,* edited by Marita Golden, 113–26. New York: Doubleday, 1993.
  Campbell focuses on the marked increase in interracial marriages involving black men and white women. She furthermore expounds on the "brainwashing" process that has caused many Asian, Latino, and Jewish men to have a preference for blonde white women.

_____. "Blacks Who Live in a White World." *Ebony* (Mar. 1982): 141–42, 144–46.
  Examining the ways that blacks must adjust when working in the upper echelons of predominantly white companies, Campbell asserts that loss of identity is not necessarily a consequence.

_____. *Brothers and Sisters.* New York: Putnam, 1994.
  Beneath the surface of this novel about the banking industry lie deep truths about relationships between women and men, and blacks and whites. Among other things, the novel examines sexism, racism, and the nature of corporate competition when affirmative action looms as a perpetual concern.

_____. "Polishing Your Business Image." *Essence* (Mar. 1984): 89, 125–26, 128.
  Stipulating that corporations are conservative entities, Campbell gives advice on how to dress and how to project an effective communication style.

_____. *Your Blues Ain't Like Mine.* 1992. New York: Ballantine, 1993.
   This novel is largely based on the Emmett Till lynching that occurred in 1955 in Mississippi. In what amounts to a riveting psychological study, the author reflects on social conditions that likely influenced the lynchers.

Christian, Barbara. "Gloria Naylor's Geography: Community, Class, and Patriarchy in *The Women of Brewster Place* and *Linden Hills.*" In *Reading Black, Reading Feminist,* edited by Henry Louis Gates, 348–73. New York: Meridian, 1990.
   An investigation of the racial, cultural, and socioeconomic factors that cause blacks to be located in specific geographical areas. Christian notes that while residents of the Brewster Place housing project are mostly transient women, Linden Hills's inhabitants are relatively stationary soulless men.

Cose, Ellis. "Caught Between Two Worlds: Why Simpson Couldn't Overcome the Barriers of Race." *Newsweek* (July 11, 1994): 28.
   Prior to the murders of Nicole Brown Simpson and Ronald Goldman, O. J. Simpson had desired that color not be a factor in how the public perceived him. But the tragedy of the murders caused America to reassess how race has been a factor not only for Simpson but for society as a whole.

_____. *The Rage of a Privileged Class.* New York: HarperCollins, 1993.
   Many blacks have found a measure of success in the white corporate world. But upon interviewing some of these black employees, Cose uncovered mounting frustration due to resentment over affirmative action, presumptions of inferiority, and limitations on professional advancement that exist in the corporate work place.

Davis, George, and Glegg Watson. *Black Life in Corporate America: Swimming in the Mainstream.* New York: Anchor, 1982.
   Davis and Watson trace the evolution of black managers in white corporations from the early 1950s to the early 1980s. For workers in general, competence and performance are often less important than politics, personality, and personal contacts. Survival can be especially difficult for blacks as they negotiate those subtle complexities.

Davis, Ossie. "On Malcolm X" (afterword). In *The Autobiography of Malcolm X,* by Malcolm X and Alex Haley, 457–60. New York: Grove, 1966.
   An acclaimed actor explains why he eulogized Malcolm X. In an era when it still was thought that blacks should be timid, Malcolm X unabashedly declared his manhood. Davis thus felt compelled to pay tribute to one who did not hesitate to make the ultimate sacrifice.

Deutsch, Leonard. "Ralph Waldo Ellison and Ralph Waldo Emerson: A Shared Moral Vision." *CLA Journal* 16 (1972): 159–78.
There is much to be said about the power of naming. Noting that Ellison's parents named him after Emerson, Deutsch examines the ways in which Emersonian philosophy influenced Ellison's writing. Though the novelist drew heavily on the theme of self-reliance, he was far less inclined to view the world as naturally harmonious.

Du Bois, W.E.B. *The Souls of Black Folk.* 1903. Greenwich, Connecticut: Fawcett, 1961.
An assessment of the progress that blacks had made leading up to the twentieth century. Numerous cultural and historical perspectives are offered; however, perhaps most significant is Du Bois's characterization of Booker T. Washington as an accommodationist whose industrial education approach actually hampered black social and political progress.

Dunbar, Paul Laurence. "We Wear the Mask." In *The Complete Poems of Paul Laurence Dunbar*, 112–13. New York: Dodd, 1948.
The mask is a metaphor for the tactics of deception that have been employed by blacks from the time of slavery to the present. Frederick Douglass, Ralph Ellison, and others have also elaborated on this phenomenon in their writing, since pretense is often the best way for a despised underclass to guarantee its survival.

Ellison, Ralph. "Hidden Name and Complex Fate." 1964. In *Shadow and Act*, 144–66. New York: Vintage, 1972.
Ellison ponders the process whereby one becomes a writer. In his own case, the fact that he was named after Ralph Waldo Emerson was especially significant. The novelist also acknowledges African American folk culture as a profound influence.

_____. *Invisible Man.* 1952. New York: Vintage, 1972.
Through the use of a nameless narrator, Ellison investigates the circumstances whereby certain individuals are rendered virtually invisible. While on one level the novel is about the rites of passage of a young black man, on another level the book raises questions concerning the extent to which a much larger segment of society goes unnoticed in the course of human events. Arguably the best novel written in the twentieth century, it canvasses a wide variety of issues including folklore, college life, the business world, and political action.

_____. "The Little Man at Chehaw Station." In *Going to the Territory*, 3–38. New York: Random, 1986.

In the mid–1930s, Ellison encountered a smallish man behind a stove in an obscure train station. The writer now considers how this man is an appropriate metaphor for a less-than-sophisticated audience demanding nevertheless to be considered in the literary interpretational process.

_____. "What America Would Be Like Without Blacks." In *Going to the Territory*, 104–12. New York: Random, 1986.

Thomas Jefferson and Abraham Lincoln were two of many who believed that the solution to America's race problem was to ship blacks back to Africa. Ellison, on the other hand, explains how if that had been done, American culture as we know it would not exist.

Emerson, Ralph Waldo. "The American Scholar." In *Ralph Waldo Emerson*, edited by Richard Poirer, 37–52. New York: Oxford University Press, 1990.

Emerson sets the conditions whereby an individual might best achieve intellectual development. An understanding of the past, a love for nature, selective reclusion, and action based on high principles are all essential if the process is to be successful.

_____. "Experience." In *Ralph Waldo Emerson*, edited by Richard Poirer, 216–34. New York: Oxford University Press, 1990.

Emerson argues against the notion that a life best lived is filled with certainty. Instead, the philosopher-poet insists that life's inconsistencies should give us the greatest joy and spur us on to vast individualistic accomplishments.

_____. "Self-Reliance." In *Ralph Waldo Emerson*, edited by Richard Poirer, 131–51. New York: Oxford University Press, 1990.

Urging against blind conformity, Emerson offers Socrates, Copernicus, Galileo, and others as examples of men who remained committed to unique perspectives in spite of a disbelieving society. Faith in one's own instincts is at the core of this essay that served as a source for Ellison's *Invisible Man*.

Ewing, Jon. "The Great Tenure Battle of 1977" (interview with Ishmael Reed). In *Shrovetide in Old New Orleans*, edited by Ishmael Reed, 219–36.

In this interview, Reed explains why he was denied tenure in the English Department at the University of California at Berkeley. His interracial marriage, pro-African perspectives, and unwillingness to socialize seem to have been more at issue than his teaching and writing accomplishments.

Frazier, E. Franklin. *Black Bourgeoisie.* 1957. New York: Free Press, 1965.
This noted sociologist characterizes the black middle class as embroiled in a major dilemma. While striving to belong to a white world that will not accept them, the black bourgeoisie seeks to be separate from the lower classes of the black race. The result is isolation and a subsequent inferiority complex.

Gaines, Patrice. *Laughing in the Dark.* New York: Crown, 1994.
A young black woman evolves through a series of tragic experiences to become a staff reporter for *The Washington Post.* Involvement with drugs and time in jail comprise significant phases of Gaines's life story.

Gates, Henry Louis. *Figures in Black.* New York: Oxford University Press, 1989.
Gates examines a wide variety of African American writers, from Phillis Wheatley to Ishmael Reed. In his first chapter, he supplies a rationale whereby theoretical perspectives might be included in analyses of African American literature.

_____. *The Signifying Monkey: A Theory of Afro-American Literary Criticism.* New York: Oxford University Press, 1988.
Gates explores the ways in which more recent black writers, in creating their own texts, have been revising the works of their literary predecessors.

_____. "'What's Love Got to Do with It?': Critical Theory, Integrity, and the Black Idiom." *New Literary History* 18 (1987): 345–62.
Gates's vitriolic response to Joyce A. Joyce's accusation that he eliminates race from consideration even as he analyzes black literature. Gates contends that as a literary critic it is not his objective to lead black people to freedom.

Gomes, Ralph, and Linda Faye Williams. "Race and Crime: The Role of the Media in Perpetuating Racism and Classism in America." In *Sources: Notable Selections in Race and Ethnicity,* edited by Adalberto Aguirre and David Baker, 337–46. Guilford, Connecticut: Dushkin, 1995.
Race and class determine to a large extent how the media will portray criminal activity. Street crimes typically are sensationalized while white-collar crimes are presented more sympathetically, if they are reported at all.

Graham, Lawrence Otis. *Member of the Club.* New York: HarperCollins, 1995.
A Harvard-trained lawyer recounts how his impeccable credentials were still not enough to gain him admission into an affluent Connecticut

country club. He only got in by applying to be a busboy. Additional chapters in this book further convey the shocking reality of race relations near the close of the twentieth century.

Grier, William, and Price Cobbs. *Black Rage.* 1968. New York: Basic, 1992.

Two psychiatrists analyze the psychological impacts of racism on blacks in America. Issues involving religion, sexuality, education, and the law are included.

Harris, Joel Chandler. "How Mr. Rabbit Was Too Sharp for Mr. Fox." In *Uncle Remus: His Songs and His Sayings*, 29–31. New York: D. Appleton, 1881.

This tale features two of folklore's most endearing characters, Brer Rabbit and Brer Fox. As told by Uncle Remus, Brer Rabbit is able to escape from the clutches of Brer Fox by insisting that being flung into a brier-patch would be a horrible fate. Wanting to hurt the rabbit as much as possible, the fox flings him into the patch. But as it turns out, the rabbit is as much at home in the brier-patch as anywhere else in the world.

Heller, Joseph. *Something Happened.* New York: Knopf, 1974.

The existential tale of Bob Slocum whose problems include an unhappy wife, unhappy children, unhappy subordinates on the job, and a United States government that is increasingly becoming inept. He rails against blind conformity, but then eventually submits to it. When he kills his son near the end of the novel, it is unclear if it was accidental or the intentional act of a father wishing to spare his child the agony of a meaningless existence.

Hernton, Calvin. *Sex and Racism in America.* 1965. New York: Anchor, 1992.

Due to the particular course of American history, issues of racism and sexuality are inextricably linked. Devoting one chapter each to black women, black men, white women, and white men, Hernton explores how racist laws, social taboos, and socially imposed ideas of beauty have left many Americans in a state of virtual psychosis.

Homans, Margaret. "The Woman in the Cave: Recent Feminist Fictions and the Classical World." *Contemporary Literature* 29 (1988): 387.

Homans relies on Plato, Dante, and Virgil's interpretations of the underworld as she elaborates on feminist writers whose women protagonists are trapped in dire situations. An extensive analysis of Gloria Naylor's *Linden Hills* is included.

hooks, bell. *Ain't I a Woman*. 1981. Boston: South End, 1992.
    An investigation of the status of black women from slavery through the 1970s. hooks examines in particular the impacts of the feminist movement, black male oppression, and white male patriarchy.

_____. "Appearance Obsession: Is the Price Too High?" *Essence* (Aug. 1995): 69–70, 112.
    Society teaches women what they must do in order to be regarded as beautiful. The task can be especially daunting for black women who aspire to a standard that is essentially based on a white aesthetic.

Huie, William Bradford. "The Shocking Story of Approved Killing in Mississippi." *Look* (Jan. 24, 1956): 46–48, 50.
    An account of the lynching of 14-year-old Emmett Till in 1955 in Mississippi. The killers were found not guilty by an all-male white jury.

Hurston, Zora Neale. *Their Eyes Were Watching God*. 1937. New York: Perennial, 1990.
    This novel traces the development of Janie Crawford from the time when she was a teenager to the point where she is a middle-aged woman. The major lesson she learns is that a person's identity is sacred, to be shaped by the individual.

Jacobs, Harriet. *Incidents in the Life of a Slave Girl*. 1861. Cambridge: Harvard University Press, 1987.
    An escaped slave recounts her experiences in bondage. For years, her owner had sexually harassed her, and then upon her escape, he became obsessed with her capture.

Johnson, James Weldon. *The Autobiography of an Ex-Coloured Man*. 1912. New York: Hill and Wang, 1981.
    A light-skinned black man has a choice of either living in the black world or crossing over and pretending he is white.

Joyce, Joyce A. "'Who the Cap Fit': Unconsciousness and Unconscionableness in the Criticism of Houston A. Baker, Jr., and Henry Louis Gates, Jr." *New Literary History* 18 (1987): 371–84.
    A critique of how Baker and Gates use Eurocentric theorists to elucidate black culture. Joyce accuses those two black critics of being paternalistic, misogynist, paranoid, and elitist.

Kaufman, Jonathan. "Black Executives Say Prejudice Still Impedes Their Path to the Top." *The Wall Street Journal* (July 9, 1980): 1, 21.

An assessment of the status of blacks at the executive level of corporate America. Often black vice presidents hold positions in public relations or personnel, highly visible posts but not very promising in terms of the prospects for future advancement.

Kirschenman, Joleen, and Kathryn Neckerman. "'We'd Love to Hire Them, But …': The Meaning of Race for Employers." In *The Urban Underclass*, edited by Christopher Jencks and Paul Peterson, 203–31. Washington, D.C.: Brookings Institution, 1991.

A study based on interviews conducted during 1988 and 1989, with employers in the Chicago area. Many of the employers expressed a reluctance to hire blacks due to a stereotypical perception of them as unmotivated, unskilled, and illiterate.

Lawlor, Julia. "Executive Exodus." *Working Woman* (Nov. 1994): 38–41, 80, 82–83, 87.

Lawlor describes a "corporate culture" that is generally unfriendly to executive women. The mere presence of high-level women makes some male managers uncomfortable. Rather than continue working in such an environment, many women executives resign their positions and seek opportunities elsewhere.

Leatherman, Courtney. "Abolition of Tenure Rattles Faculty at College of Ozarks." *The Chronicle of Higher Education* (Jan. 26, 1994): A18-A19.

An account of how one academic institution eliminated tenure within the ranks of its faculty members. Board of Trustee members who defend the action argue that no other business guarantees lifetime employment. Many faculty members, on the other hand, express concern about the impact on academic freedom.

Lee, Jo Ann. "Special Problems of Older Gay Employees." In *Homosexual Issues in the Workplace*, edited by Louis Diamant, 217–23. Washington, D.C.: Taylor and Francis, 1993.

Generally speaking, homosexuals have to negotiate a complex path in order to achieve success in the workplace. The strategy often chosen is one of concealing the fact that they are homosexual. Coming out of the closet poses special difficulties for older homosexuals since they were raised in a more socially restrictive era.

Lewis, Reginald, and Blair Walker. *"Why Should White Guys Have All the Fun?": How Reginald Lewis Created a Billion-Dollar Business Empire*. New York: John Wiley, 1995.

As a determined undergraduate student at Virginia State College,

Lewis laid the groundwork whereby he would later gain admission into Harvard Law School. Upon graduation, he went to work for a New York City law firm, but soon realized that his prospects for great success could only be realized if he went into business for himself. His persistence and business acumen reached legendary stature once he gained control of TLC Beatrice International, Inc. and became one of the wealthiest black men in America.

Lewis, Sinclair. *Babbitt*. San Diego: Harcourt, 1922.
Aspiring to be the quintessential businessman, Babbitt later learns that in the midst of this quest, he has lost his individuality.

London, Jack. "The Unparalleled Invasion." In *The Strength of the Strong*, 71–100. New York: MacMillan, 1914.
In this futuristic allegory, London portrays China as an uncontrollably large population spilling over its own borders and conquering adjacent countries and territories. Nations of the Western world respond by joining together in a plan of genocide that, once put into effect, obliterates the Chinese people.

_____. "The Yellow Peril." In *Revolution and Other Essays*, 269–89. New York: MacMillan, 1910.
London professes the superiority of the Anglo-Saxon race and proclaims the Japanese as a threat to civilization.

Lorde, Audre. "The Master's Tools Will Never Dismantle the Master's House." In *Sister Outsider: Essays and Speeches*, 110–13. Trumansburg, New York: Crossing Press, 1984.
Lorde laments that at a recent New York University humanities conference, there was only one panel in which black lesbian feminist perspectives were included. From that experience, Lorde concludes that the world of academia is without the wherewithal to effectively address the concerns of lesbians, blacks, and the poor.

McCall, Nathan. *Makes Me Wanna Holler: A Young Black Man in America*. New York: Random, 1994.
A young black journalist retraces the course of an eventful life that took him from violence and incarceration to employment as a reporter for *The Washington Post*.

McClenney, Earl. *How to Survive When You're the Only Black in the Office*. Richmond, Virginia: First Associates, 1987.
An advice book for black men who work in a predominantly white

office setting. Caution is the key. In such a situation one must calculate carefully what to wear, when to socialize, and, when the issue presents itself, whether or not to file a grievance.

McPherson, James Alan. "Indivisible Man." *The Atlantic Monthly* (Dec. 1970): 45–60.

McPherson uses conversations, interviews, letters, and lectures to uncover something of the essence of the novelist Ralph Ellison.

Malcolm X. "Message to the Grass Roots." In *Malcolm X Speaks*, edited by George Breitman, 3–17. 1965. New York: Grove, 1966.

Speaking in Detroit in 1963, Malcolm X laid the ground rules for a social revolution. He distinguished himself from other black leaders of his time, and drew on a slavery analogy, characterizing himself as a field Negro likely to be betrayed by house Negroes such as the ones who earlier that year had participated in the March on Washington.

Meier, August, and Elliott Rudwick. *Black Detroit and the Rise of the UAW*. 1979. New York: Oxford University Press, 1981.

A history of the black community in Detroit in light of the emergence of the automobile industry and the United Auto Workers union.

Miller, Arthur. *Death of a Salesman*. 1949. New York: Viking, 1971.

At one time a successful salesman, Willy Loman, in old age, has outlived his usefulness to the company where he had worked for almost four decades. Dreams that he had for his children have not come to fruition and he ultimately chooses suicide over acknowledging that his vision of life was a failure.

Molloy, John T. *Dress for Success*. New York: Peter Wyden, 1975.

A practical guide on how to dress in order to succeed in the business world. In his straightforward chapter entitled "Some Advice for Minorities," Molloy acknowledges that white men have an advantage in the image game. Consequently, blacks and other minorities have to be especially conservative in their dress in order to succeed at the highest corporate levels.

Mullings, Leith. "Images, Ideology, and Women of Color." In *Women of Color in U.S. Society*, edited by Maxine Baca Zinn and Bonnie Thornton Dill, 265–89. Philadelphia: Temple University Press, 1994.

Mullings explains how current stereotypes of black women have their roots in the institution of American slavery. Stereotypical attitudes about women of color in general make socioeconomic advancement for them a difficult proposition.

Naylor, Gloria. *Bailey's Cafe*. 1992. New York: Vintage, 1993.

In this novel of mythical proportion, Naylor describes a cafe that is at once a dining facility and a refuge for social outcasts. Prominent among these individuals is Miss Maple, a man who dresses in women's clothing as he goes on job interviews.

_____. *Linden Hills*. 1985. New York: Penguin, 1986.

An all-black community has the appearance of prosperity and contentment. In actuality, there is an evil involved concerning the undertaker Luther Nedeed and his male successors. Relying substantially on Dante's *Inferno* as a frame of reference for her novel, Naylor exposes the quest for social status as a struggle in which certain individuals compromise themselves to the extent where they lose their very souls.

_____. *The Women of Brewster Place*. 1982. New York: Penguin, 1983.

A collection of stories about black women struggling for sustenance and dignity amidst the poverty of an inner-city housing project.

Nelson, Jill. *Volunteer Slavery*. Chicago: Noble, 1993.

Nelson recounts her experiences as a writer for the Sunday magazine section of *The Washington Post*. She comes to the realization that she was not so much hired to produce articles as she was hired to serve as a token who would support the newspaper, however questionable its actions might be.

Osborn, John Jay. *The Paper Chase*. 1971. New York: Avon, 1973.

Osborn follows the activities of several students in their first year at Harvard Law School. Much of the novel focuses on the stern Professor Kingsfield and his use of the Socratic teaching method.

Parini, Jay. "Tenure and the Loss of Faculty Talent." *The Chronicle of Higher Education* (July 14, 1995): A40.

A professor of English at Middlebury College assesses the system of tenure in higher education. Good teachers are often sacrificed because they do not meet the standard for publications, a standard that interestingly enough can vary from one year to another at the same institution and with regard to the same tenure candidate. Parini urges untenured faculty to keep quiet about controversial issues so as to avoid a negative tenure vote that might in actuality be a plot for revenge carried out to fruition.

Rampersad, Arnold. Introduction to *Native Son*, by Richard Wright. 1940. New York: HarperPerennial, 1993.

Rampersad introduces this new edition of the novel as Wright had initially intended it. Certain sexually explicit scenes were excluded when the work first appeared in 1940.

Reed, Ishmael. *The Free-Lance Pallbearers.* 1967. New Jersey: Chatham, 1975.
Reed examines a wide range of issues involving religion, academia, and politics. The experimental style of this first novel is a telling trademark serving notice for what will be a persistent existentialism in subsequent works by the author.

_____. "Hoodoo Manifesto #2 on Criticism: The Baker-Gayle Fallacy." *Umum Newsletter* 4 (1975): 8–11.
Using literary critic Houston Baker as an example, Reed lambastes members of the black intelligentsia for their adherence to Western culture.

_____. *Japanese by Spring.* New York: Atheneum, 1993.
Benjamin Puttbutt, a black professor at a predominantly white college, aspires to achieve tenure and behaves in such a fashion so as to win the approval of his senior colleagues. What he learns, however, is that those colleagues have little or no allegiance to him even though he desperately seeks to fit in.

Russell, Kathy, Midge Wilson, and Ronald Hall. *The Color Complex: The Politics of Skin Color Among African Americans.* 1992. New York: Anchor, 1993.
White discrimination against blacks is a well-documented feature of American society. But now these authors provide the extensive details for how blacks discriminate against other blacks on the basis of different skin color.

Salinger, J.D. *The Catcher in the Rye.* 1951. New York: Bantam, 1981.
The main protagonist, Holden Caulfield, is disturbed by the phoniness he sees in adults. A major question arises concerning whether his feelings are typical of adolescents or proof that he is maladjusted. Since the novel is an indictment against institutions, it is useful to consider that the author himself attended military school and then later attended several colleges, but received no college degree.

Thornbrough, Emma. "Booker T. Washington as Seen by His White Contemporaries." *The Journal of Negro History* 53 (1968): 161–82.
Though some whites detested Washington simply because he was a black man, many other whites applauded his work at Tuskegee Institute. Supporters included prominent Americans such as the writer William Dean Howells, Presidents Theodore Roosevelt and William Howard Taft, and industrialist Andrew Carnegie.

Turow, Scott. *One L.* 1977. New York: Penguin, 1983.
An account of the first-year experiences of Turow and others who attended Harvard Law School during the mid–1970s.

United States Department of Labor, Women's Bureau. *Working Women Count!* Washington, D.C.: Department of Labor, 1994.
In 1994, the Women's Bureau of the United States Department of Labor surveyed over a quarter of a million working women and found that disproportionate salaries and unequal opportunity for advancement were among their major concerns.

Wade, Brent. *Company Man.* 1992. New York: Anchor, 1993.
The chronicle of a black man's precipitous rise through the ranks of a predominantly white corporation. He becomes a top executive but pays a steep price as his corporate superiors expect him to act in such a manner that amounts to him selling his soul.

Walker, Alice. "If the Present Looks Like the Past, What Does the Future Look Like?" 1982. In *In Search of Our Mothers' Gardens*, 290–312. San Diego: Harvest, 1983.
In this essay originally published in *Essence* magazine under the title "Embracing the Dark and the Light," Walker voices concern about how the black race remains color conscious.

Washington, Booker T. *Up From Slavery.* 1901. New York: Bantam, 1970.
One of America's greatest leaders tells of his meteoric rise from slave to president of Tuskegee Institute in Alabama.

Watkins, Mel. "An Interview with Ishmael Reed." *The Southern Review* 21 (1985): 603–14.
In assessing black literature, Reed criticizes the situation of East Coast intellectuals deciding which works will get published and promoted.

Westkott, Marcia. "Women's Studies as a Strategy for Change: Between Criticism and Vision." In *Theories of Women's Studies*, edited by Gloria Bowles and Renate Duelli Klein, 210–18. Boston: Routledge, 1983.
The college classroom should be a venue for essential discussions about women's issues. However, certain traditional methodologies may first have to be dismantled.

"White Male Executives Haven't Changed Ways." *Jet* (June 21, 1993): 28.
Most companies have regulations against racism and sexism. Yet, executives still make personnel decisions based on whether they can identify

with the job candidate, which means that the issue of diversity still is often ignored.

Whitman, Walt. "Earth, My Likeness." In *Complete Poetry and Selected Prose*, edited by James E. Miller, 96. Boston: Houghton Mifflin, 1959.
With nature as a backdrop, Whitman explores issues of homosexuality. The poem provides clues to what might have been the author's own homosexuality.

_____. "To a Stranger." In *Complete Poetry and Selected Prose*, edited by James E. Miller, 93. Boston: Houghton Mifflin, 1959.
Reflecting on one who might be an ideal mate, Whitman progresses from characterizing that person as a stranger to characterizing that individual as one with whom he has shared profound intimacies.

_____. "What Think You I Take My Pen in Hand?" In *Complete Poetry and Selected Prose*, edited by James E. Miller, 97. Boston: Houghton Mifflin, 1959.
In this contemplative poem, Whitman posits a variety of subjects about which he could write — the splendors of nature, the sprawl of a city, or the majesty of a battleship. However, he rejects those possibilities and elaborates instead on the beauty of a relationship between two men.

Wilkins, David. "Two Paths to the Mountaintop?: The Role of Legal Education in Shaping the Values of Black Corporate Lawyers." *Standard Law Review* 45 (1993): 1981–2026.
Wilkins assesses what the role of law schools should be in preparing black students for the moral paradoxes with which they are likely to be confronted. Excellent employment opportunities await such students, but also the prospect that they will be assisting companies in perpetuating conditions not in the best interests of the black community.

Wright, Richard. *Lawd Today*. 1963. New York: Avon, 1969.
Published posthumously, this novel recounts the events of one day in the life of a post office worker. Wright uses existentialist technique to portray a world that, though bustling with activity, remains essentially meaningless.

Index

DATE DUE
